THE ODESK REVOLUTION

© 2014 Michael Marcovici

ISBN 9783735720559

„Herstellung und Verlag: BoD – Books on Demand, Norderstedt"

Bibliografische Information der Deutschen Nationalbibliothek: Die Deutsche Nationalbibliothek verzeichnet diese Publikation in der Deutschen Nationalbibliografie; detaillierte bibliografische Daten sind im Internet über **www.dnb.de** abrufbar.

FREELANCING ONLINE
– IS IT FOR YOU?

There has been a massive boom in freelance working in recent years and online or virtual projects have taken more than a fair share of the business. But is it a good idea for either the worker or the employer to get involved in this area? Is it more trouble than it is worth and do many people on both sides of the arrangement just end up getting burned?

In researching this book (and in my own experience) I have come to the conclusion that it is worthwhile and, while there are unscrupulous individuals in both camps - client and employee – they are in the great minority; and there are subtle ways of spotting the scammers plus safeguards you can take advantage of.

Freelancing does bring tangible benefits to both parties in the contract. The client gets to choose from a wide pool of talent and can change the contractor dependent on the type of job. They don't have to directly employ them and pay all the consequent oncosts; and they can terminate the agreement whenever they like. For the contractor they have a range of clients to pitch at, can please themselves how much or how little they bid for and when and how they do the work (up to a point!). They can also expect a much wider variety of work than they would probably get in an ordinary 9-5 job. The internet has only increased the

range and geographical scope of the market and made virtual work a truly international option.

Of course there are downsides as well. You have to get the work in the first place and both clients and contractors can misrepresent themselves in all sorts of ways. Often payment is at the discretion of the client and unscrupulous clients can use websites to get work done for free or very little if they are smart and manipulative enough. Luckily these people usually get rumbled and weeded out but you do need to be alert to the possibility of being cheated.

The compilation that follows tries to look at all aspects of online freelancing – from the reasons for, and ways of, doing it to the best sites for various disciplines; and looking at the pitfalls and benefits along the way. We do not recommend online freelancing – nor warn against it. Nor do we vouch for any of the sites, techniques or sources described here. They might be good or useful – they might not. We are just providing information and insight into the subject so you can decide whether you want to know more and proceed – or come to the conclusion that you wouldn't touch it with a bargepole. Both views can be valid; it is not for everyone.

If you are interested this will be a useful starting point and a reference source to begin your research and learning on the subject. If you decide it is for you, good luck with your search. It can be an exciting and fulfilling ride if you go in with the right attributes and attitude.

Back blurb

The recent boom in freelancing has only been enhanced and expanded by the global availability that the internet providesand many have turned to the web as either client or contractor to get the best possible options for jobs. Around the millennium entrepreneurs began to catch on to the business potential of this latent supply and demand and online freelancing sites such as elance and odesk sprang up. They have thrived and cater for hundreds of thousands of jobs and people today. This book looks at freelancing as a concept – the advantages and pitfalls, the pros and cons. It also looks at the plethora of websites offering this type of opportunity for different disciplines such as writing, computing, design and admin work. We are not recommending online freelance as a life style nor any of the sites or techniques mentioned. What we are doing is providing a useful introduction to the subject and a rich information source so you can decide yourself whether this is for you. Good hunting!

CONTENTS

1

General Freelancing Information

Tips & Insights Into Online Freelancing

Introduction to Freelancing

Freelancing is one of the very best ways to make a bit of money if you are a college or university student. Likewise, any other young people who are out of work but have access to the internet can make decent money doing online freelancing using skills they already have – or skills that they can improve over the internet.

What Is Online Freelancing?

Online freelancing is carrying out tasks that other people don't have the time, inclination or skills to carry out themselves. If you have spare time and access to the internet at home or elsewhere then you can use your skills to make money freelancing online.

How Does Online Freelancing Work?

Freelance work from home Typically, someone will post a job or project on an online freelance website and interested freelancers will bid on the job. They say how much they would charge to complete the task and why they are the best person to carry it out.

Often, these proposals are 'sealed' so that only the hirer can see the full details of all of the proposals – the aim being to prevent providers trying to undercut the bids that other freelancers have already been placed.

The person who posted the task then chooses from all of the proposals that they've received and awards the job to the cheapest provider or the freelancer they consider to be the best-qualified for the task.

The freelancer then carries out the work and sends the completed project back to the hirer. If both parties are agreed that the project has been carried out in a suitable manner then payment will be facilitated.

What Sort Of Work Is Available?

There is a wide variety of work available that can be carried out online so you should be able to find at least a few things that you could perform as a freelancer.

Just some of the projects you could bid on include:

- *Article Writing*
- *Graphic Design*
- *Proofreading*
- *Editing*
- *Online Research*
- *Programming*
- *Copywriting*
- *Transcription*

- *Translation*
- *Data Entry*
- *Spreadsheet Work*
- *Virtual Personal Assistant*
- *Data Analysis*

1,000's of jobs on oDesk

Basically, the list is endless. If you have a skill that is in demand, then there's a good chance that someone out there will be posting tasks looking for someone just like you.

How Do Online Freelancers Get Paid?

Often, as soon as the task is completed and both parties are agreed that everything is okay, the job is marked as complete and the hirer will pay over the agreed amount to the freelancer.

Some freelance websites or particular tasks involve an 'Escrow' system which aims to guarantee upfront that both parties will be happy with how the job is completed. Usually, the hirer pays the money to the freelance website as soon as the job is awarded and they hold the funds until the job is marked as complete and everyone is happy. In the event of any dispute, the freelance website will arbitrate before the money is either paid over to the provider or refunded to the hirer.

Yet other tasks can be carried out on an hourly basis where you 'clock in' to the freelance website while you are working and invoices are produced based on the number of hours you've actually been working on the project.

The money builds up in your online freelance account until it reaches a minimum payout level, at which point the freelance site will either send the money over to your bank account, send out a cheque, or pay you via PayPal etc.

Some of the freelance sites also produce credit card style cards which they will send to you and which can subsequently be 'loaded' with your freelance earnings.

What Are The Best Freelance Websites?

There are loads of freelance websites to choose from – and all of them have their plus points and minus points. Some are better for beginners who are looking to get their first freelance job online. Others are better for students or young people who have more advanced skills or who already have a few online freelance projects under their belt.

On balance, some of the best websites for online freelance work that we have found include:

- **Elance**
- **Guru**
- **oDesk**
- **Freelancer.com**
- **People Per Hour**
- **Clickworker**
- **Fiverr.com**

If you've never done any online freelance work before then it's worth taking a bit of time to browse through all of these websites to see what sort of jobs or projects are available and which sites have the sort of work that best matches your particular skill set or strong points.

Also, try to work out the fee structures for the different websites. It's best to know exactly how much of the amount you bid for the job is actually going to hit your account.

How To Stand Out From The Crowd As A Freelancer

Complete Your Profile

One of the most important things you can do if you want to be successful as an online freelancer is to fill your profile out properly and make it stand out from the crowd.

All too often you see freelance websites littered with freelancer profiles containing nothing more than a name and a tiny bit of education background. Would you hire someone based on a profile like that?

No – so don't leave your own online profile incomplete or nobody is going to award a job to you.

Highlight Your Skills

As you would with a real-world CV, spend a bit of time filling out something about yourself in every single profile field that you can, and give reasons why you should be hired for the freelance contract rather than someone else.

What are your unique selling points? Are you simply the best programmer around? Is your spelling and grammar much better than the average user of the website? If so, then let potential employers know that on your profile – and back it up with evidence.

Add a Photo

Always make the effort to add a profile photo of yourself. Most contractors won't even notice a profile with the bog standard default profile image, so upload a good photo of yourself looking friendly, professional – and very hireable!

Get Good Feedback

Whenever you manage to secure a freelance job and successfully complete it, make sure you try to get the hirer to leave some good feedback on your profile about you. Getting strong testimonies from previous job awarders is one of the best ways to make sure your freelancer profile looks impressive to potential future job awarders.

Take Free Skills Tests

Some of the online freelance sites allow you to carry out free skills tests to display your proficiency at certain tasks on your profile. For example, you might see a free skill test about spelling and grammar. If you are hoping to get freelance work writing articles or proofreading then make sure you carry out those sorts of free tests to give potential hirers one more reason to pick you rather than someone else.

Some Pitfalls of Freelancing – and How to Avoid Them

Bidding On Jobs You Can't Actually Do

If you don't think you could carry out a task in a way that is going to satisfy the hirer, then it's probably best not to even make a bid proposal in the first place. If the hirer isn't happy with the work you send back to them, then it's only going to lead to disputed payments and negative feedback. You don't need that sort of things at any stage of your freelancing career.

Bidding Too High At The Start

With online freelancing you often need to start out with very low bid prices just to get yourself noticed. Too many people over-value their skills at the beginning and are left disappointed because they are never awarded any jobs.

Once you've get a few cheap jobs behind you, and have built up your profile with great feedback from previous hirers, then you can start to raise your prices. Some hirers will be prepared to pay more for jobs when they can see that you've already managed to complete tasks to the satisfaction of other hirers.

Not Checking Out The Hirer's Profile

The majority of people who post jobs on freelance websites are honest hirers who just want to get a task completed to the standard they require.

As you would expect, though, unfortunately there are a few unscrupulous hirers who try to take advantage of the system to get work completed for free by freelancers. They either just refuse to pay the freelancer or they create enough of a dispute and the threat of negative feedback that the freelancer would rather just walk away.

Luckily, a quick look over the hirer's profile will help you decide whether or not to trust them. Ask yourself a few questions to put your mind at rest before you even make a bid. Has the hirer posted jobs previously? Did they award the jobs to a provider? Was payment made? Does the hirer have a history of giving negative feedback?

Asking these questions will help you decide whether a hirer has genuine intentions about the jobs they are posting. And the good news is that the vast majority of hirers do have genuine intentions.

Online Freelance Work – Some Takeaways

Have a look over the freelance websites we picked out above or try to find some niche freelance websites if you have a particular skill that might be much in demand

Sign up for an account with all of the freelance websites that you feel most suit you and give you the best chance of finding work

Fill out your profile as much as possible

Start bidding on jobs

Start earning money as an online freelancer!

http://www.e4s.co.uk/jobs/1-freelance-jobs-for-students.htm

HOW TO MAKE AN IMPRESSIVE FREELANCE PORTFOLIO

Posted in <u>Freelance</u>, <u>How To</u> By <u>admin</u>

If freelancing or online earning is your interest then, it is good news for you because there are innumerable opportunities that enable you to work from home. Of course, not all the freelancing jobs are knocking your doors in the beginning, in fact, you have to ignite your efforts and time in the start of your career.

Just like the regular job, in <u>online job</u> you have to show your resume to present your experience and skills to qualify for the applied position. To better impress the potential employers and in freelancing job we named them clients, you have to present them with your portfolio or a comprehensive summary of your entire freelancing potentials.

Mostly freelance jobs require the freelancers to work from the ease of home through the internet that is why making a strong portfolio you steps ahead of the competitors for the applied post.

Where to go for portfolios?

There are some reliable and good sites that offer free account to start your freelancing career (In case you've no idea on how to start a promising freelance career and which freelance site to choose, then you'd find tutorials at the end of this article). They offer ample room to build a strong portfolio. Moreover, you can also get your own <u>domain name</u> and hosting services for a more controlled online portfolio. Being a beginner in the freelancer race of course, you haven't got any freelance job, so you definitely think what to include in the portfolio to grasp the attention of potential clients. The content you will include in the portfolio must showcase your skills and expertise. Here are some useful tips

- o If you master the art of graphic designing then, upload some banners, images, visual designs and similar other things you have done for your personal use. But, remember it must have a professional look.
- o Being a web designer, you can easily make an attractive website to grape the needed attention.
- o Freelancers offering audio and video services can make some professional videos and can upload them easily.
- o If you are looking for <u>writing jobs</u> then, make sure all the samples you have added in the portfolio are masterpieces. Perfect spelling and grammar and the ways you advertise your skills through words make you ahead of the mob.
- o For other online jobs like project management, consulting, virtual assistance services, translation and transcription services, data entry and research you just have to add your areas of expertise and add your work experience you have up till now. But, make sure that it is relevant to the job you are eyeing. For instance, you have secretarial work experience then; you can apply for virtual assistants and administrative freelance jobs.

o   If you are in management or marketing field then, you have to apply for jobs looking for a business consultant and the project manager.

Moreover, never ever forget to add your educational background and extra certifications. Also add the years you have attended high school and university. Additionally, include the companies or organization in your portfolio you worked in the past to exhibit your expertise and credibility.

Helpful Stuff:

1. Tips to Consider while Selecting a Freelance Website
2. 3 Basic Steps For a Reliable and Promising Freelance Career

Thanks for reading it till the end. Now it's your turn! Let me know if you've any query or something to suggest or add to to what I've mentioned regarding portfolio making, just shoot it using the comment box below. I'll be more than happy to read and answer your comments. Good Luck!

http://www.earnsmartlyonline.com/2013/01/how-to-make-an-impressive-freelance-portfolio/

How to Freelance Your Expertise

If you're tired of being on the employee treadmill, now may be the best time to consider freelancing your hard-earned skills.

BY <u>ANDREA C. POE</u> |

Are dreams of freelancing dancing through your head? If you're nodding yes, now's a great time to give it a whirl. As companies scale back on their expensive, benefit-heavy workforce, they're increasingly turning to outside--freelance--help. If you've got expertise in the right areas, there's a good chance you can parlay it into a freelance career by sharing your knowledge and skills with a variety of clients.

Let Freedom Ring

There's no question about it; freelance doesn't start with the word "free" for nothing. Freedom is a major perk of freelancing. As a full-time freelancer, you'll work when you want. You can take vacations when you want, for as long as you want. Weekend getaways won't have to be confined to weekends, and business suits are mostly a thing of the past. There's no boss breathing down your neck, nagging you. And there are no irritating co-workers slacking off at the water cooler, driving you nuts.

But in exchange for all those freedoms comes risk and insecurity. As a freelancer, your next paycheck is never guaranteed. Anxiety about where the next job is coming from plagues many freelancers, no matter how seasoned. But insecurity comes with the turf, and dedicated freelancers learn to make peace with it.

The best way to ensure your freelancing future is to offer a service you know people want. Just because you'd like to do something doesn't mean that there's a readymade market for it.

"'Follow your heart and do what you love' is just a slogan. You need to get real," says Kelly James-Enger, author of *Six Figure Freelancing* . "If you're not offering a service people are willing to spend money on, you're not going to be in business [for long]."

Search your local paper and the Internet to see who's doing what you want to do, what they charge and who their clients are. Talk to everyone you know until you turn up freelancers doing what you hope to do. Then call them up and pick their brains about which segments of the market are growing and where most of their work comes from. This information is critical to helping you carve out a niche and fill a current opening in the market.

Think about this: Ten years ago, web designers made a pretty penny freelancing their services to corporations, but today the demand has lessened as all those laid-off dotcomers have created a glut in the market. On the other hand, small-business owners are more keen then ever to learn web design themselves, as are retiring baby boomers, so teaching web design may prove more lucrative than doing the actual design work right now.

Don't Quit Your Day Job--Yet

Once you've decided what aspect of your field to freelance, take the time to establish yourself. "The biggest misconception people have is that they're going to jump right into it and start making money," cautions Laurie Rozakis. "Not true. Just because you build it doesn't mean they'll come."

Rosakis, who is a freelance writer and editor, and the author of _The Complete Idiot's Guide to Making Money in Freelancing_ , says it can take months--even years--to develop a reputation and client base. For that reason, many freelancers start by moonlighting while still holding on to their day jobs.

"Everyone thinks it's going to happen overnight, but I don't know a single freelancer who immediately started making a six-figure income," maintains James-Enger.

A good rule of thumb is not to give up your day job until you have between six months and one year's worth of savings, more if you're the sole support for your household. "Don't leave your job until you're confident you can pay your mortgage and healthcare and put money into a retirement account," James-Enger advises.

Of course, moonlighting while working for your current employer can be tricky-especially if you're freelancing in the same field. Let's say you're an advertising copywriter who wants to start freelancing on the side. You'll probably need to tell your employer, who may require you to sign a noncompete agreement in which you promise not to steal, or "borrow," clients. If, on the other hand, you're an advertising copywriter who wants to do freelance Japanese translations, your employer probably doesn't even need to know what you're doing after hours.

Generating Business

As in any business, your freelancing career is only as strong as the sales you make. Finding clients is the number-one challenge for any freelancer just starting out. It's almost a catch-22: How do you attract clients when you've never had any? Here are some practical steps that will propel you out of the conundrum and into business:

1. **Develop a portfolio to demonstrate the scope of your skills.** If that means working for no pay or low pay initially, do it. Samples of your work will be your best calling card.

2. **Tell everyone you know--colleagues, friends, family, neighbors--about your new freelance gig.** Referrals will make up the bulk of your business initially.

3. **Join professional organizations--online or in the community--that serve your field.** In addition to all the other benefits you'll gain, you'll also pick up insider tips of where to find work.

4. **Join local organizations, like the chamber of commerce or Rotary club.** "Creative people often overlook organizations like these, thinking they'll be filled with stiff bankers and businesspeople," notes James-Enger. "And they may be--but that's who'll be hiring you to do your creative work."

5. **Volunteer in the community doing something you love** , and you'll broaden your network of potential clients.

6. **Cold call.** Yes, everyone hates cold calling, but the reason freelancers need to do this is because it works.

Another important point to remember is that freelancing doesn't solely mean doing the thing you love. It also means knowing how to sell and market your services. When starting out, about 90 percent of your time will be spent on sales and marketing tasks. "Work won't just stumble upon you," says James-Enger. "You can be as talented as anything, but it won't mean a thing if you can't sell yourself."

Rozakis agrees. "A lot of people go into freelancing thinking, 'I've got the talent.' What they need to realize is a lot of people have talent. What makes a successful freelance business is how strong your client list is."

And building a client base requires that you plug away tirelessly without getting discouraged. Expect rejection. It comes with the territory--and often. But don't let that stop you from trying again.

"Think of a salesperson at The Gap who gives you a pair of pants to try that don't fit," says James-Enger. "A good salesperson doesn't sulk away, dejected. She hands you another pair and another pair until you buy something."

Get Serious

When you see that you're starting to make enough money that your freelancing is becoming a viable career, it's time to start putting the business building blocks in place that will ensure that you--and your clients--take your business seriously. That means going beyond ordering hot-looking business cards.

No matter what your field, contracts are important. Many freelancers overlook developing their own, instead letting clients design contracts or foregoing them altogether. That's a mistake--and it can be a costly one.

"Protect yourself," stresses Rusty Fischer, who wrote _Freedom To Freelance_ . He recommends checking out contracts used by other freelancers you know, so you can borrow the best of what they've got and incorporate those ideas into your own contract. Then run your contract by a lawyer to make sure your rights are protected. "It's well worth a few hundred bucks to get it right," he notes.

Establishing an accounting system is also imperative. Not only will it help you keep track of what you're due, but it will simplify your life. Freelancers are on the IRS radar anyway, so good record keeping will give you peace of mind and make any possible future audit less painful.

"Get a great accountant or [take a] community college course and learn software programs like Quicken to keep your books," Rozakis recommends. "You skip this aspect of the business, and you'll be very sorry."

Depending on your industry, having a website may be helpful in marketing your services. If you have visual examples of what you do, say landscape design or theatrical costuming, a website will act as a portfolio and introduce your work to prospective clients.

(Websites are obviously less useful to freelancers without visual examples, say, home inspectors or medical billing administrators.)

Know Thy Self

One of the most important decision you'll have to make before fully committing to running a freelance business is to determine if this type of lifestyle matches your personality. "Know thyself," says Rozakis. "Really think this through before you make a commitment to a lifestyle and work style you just may not be suited for."

And while you no longer have a boss, you do have to answer to someone--yourself. That's why self-discipline is key to taking your freelancing gig from an interesting hobby to a viable business. "It really helps to be a Type A personality because you have to be able to motivate yourself and manage your time," says James-Enger. "You can't be a slacker *and* have a successful freelance career."

Tempting as it may be to cut out mid-afternoon for a movie or a walk with the dog, most days those kinds of things just aren't going to happen. "Not only will you normally work way more hours per week as a freelancer, but your schedule probably won't wind up being as flexible as you think," warns Fischer. "Most of your clients are working regular hours, from 9 to 5. Being available to them means that most of time, you'll be working very regular hours."

The freelance life is a solitary life. If you're someone who feeds off the energy of other people, freelancing may prove too lonely a road to travel. Fortunately, for those who seek them out, there are solutions to the lack of daily social contact. Many freelancers fill their need to interact with other people by taking on-site freelance gigs, where they work--at least temporarily--among other people. Others turn to freelancer support groups where they meet once a month over a cup of coffee to swap tales of glory and woe. And others work on collaborative projects with other freelancers.

It takes time to grow a freelance business; it takes time to establish yourself; and it takes time to make money. All of this can be nerve-wracking and cause countless sleepless nights. But with talent, patience, tenacity and a touch of luck, freelancing can be among the most rewarding--and lucrative--ways to make money.

"Would I ever go back to working for the 'man'?" laughs James-Enger. "No way. For all the struggles and unknowns, I wouldn't give up freelancing and be somebody's employee for anything."

Freelancing Options

Think the freelance life might be for you? The good part is, if you do it, there's a good chance you can freelance it. Here are some of the most frequently freelanced gigs around:

- Accountant/bookkeeper
- Appraiser
- Cartographer
- Chef
- Computer programmer
- Corporate event planner
- Data entry/processor
- Editor/copyeditor

- Engineer
- Esthetician
- Film animator
- Financial planner
- Floral arranger
- Fundraiser
- Furniture restorer/repairer
- Grant writer
- Graphic designer
- Home inspector
- Interior designer
- Landscape architect
- Massage therapist
- Medical administration (billing)
- Package design
- Party planner
- Photographer
- Political consultant
- Private investigator
- Professional organizer
- Sales/marketing consultant
- Seamstress
- Set designer
- Telemarketer
- Translator/interpreter
- Tutoring
- Upholsterer
- Web designer
- Writer

http://www.entrepreneur.com/article/79088

Four Online Freelancing Jobs You Should Approach with Caution

by Celine Roque
JAN. 2, 2009 - 10:00 AM PDT

First time freelancers make the mistake of accepting every single job that comes their way. I made this mistake, and there's a good chance that you did too. Who can blame us? Freelance income isn't stable, especially when you're starting out. We tend to think that we should accept all the job offers we can get today – because there might be none tomorrow.

Sometimes, however, the jobs we take end up costing us instead of giving us profits. What we intended as another step in our career only becomes a lesson we shouldn't have learned the hard way. How do we identify these problematic jobs and what can we do about them?

The Low Paying Job. These are the jobs that are often <u>advertised</u> on craigslist and they try to compensate for the low pay with promises of "exposure" or a percentage of the profits. They also make excuses, which include the following:

- they're just starting out as a company;

- web workers in developing countries charge at that low rate and you have to compete with them;
- and your pay will be increased over time (although this claim is vague and not indicated in the contract).

Even if a low paying job were legitimate, accepting it has disadvantages. This job will take hours away from your work week, hours that could be better spent on boosting your marketing efforts to get the well-paying jobs. Plus, it will lower your average hourly income overall. Ideally, you should be increasing your rates as the years go by and not the other way around.

Unless you're just starting out and looking to build your web working experience, there should be no reason to take this job.

The Job You Can't Learn From. In a previous post, Mike Gunderloy talked about how he only takes jobs that will allow him to learn something new. While I believe there's something to be learned out of every experience, I would rather take Mike's advice than accept a repetitive copy & pasting job.

Take this kind of job only if you're low on cash or if you plan to outsource or delegate it, otherwise, you won't be getting much else apart from the money.

The Audition Job. You know those jobs where you have to "audition" by doing a design mock up or a draft and if your client likes it, they'll pay you. If not, well, that's too bad. This approach to job applications is also known as speculative work (or simply "spec work"). While it's true that not all people who ask for spec work are out to scam you, it's not the best way to conduct business – both for the freelancer and the client.

The "Easy" Job. Some jobs seems simple enough when you look at your client's initial specifications, but once you get deep into the project you realize how big the scope actually is.

It's hard to identify this kind of job at first. What usually gives it away is when your client tells you "It's easy!" or "It will only take 10 minutes of your time!" Think about it, if the job were really easy, shouldn't they be able to do it themselves?

Also, while there are clients who are appreciative of a freelancer's skills and efforts, there are always those who will undervalue your work. Do you know this client well enough to trust that the job is truly easy?

One way to work through the "easy" job is to assess the project yourself, discuss it with your client, and define the deliverables before you start working. This protects you from "surprise" tasks that suddenly creep in when you realize that the scope of the project is much larger than what your client initially thought. In some way, you'll risk looking like you're out to milk your client for every penny, but if you give them all the information and references they need, they'll know that you're only doing what's best for them in the long run.

http://gigaom.com/2009/01/02/4-online-freelancing-jobs-you-should-approach-with-caution/

A WHOLE NEW WORLD

Moving on

There comes a time in your life that you simply have to walk away from that which is holding you back from fulfilling your full potential. In spring 2013, finding myself at a dead end in life, divorced and with no real way to work my way up with the company I was working for, I decided to change my career path. A friend had introduced me to the possibility of freelance writing and as I had always been a keen writer, naturally I thought to myself "I can do that!" He gave me some tips and recommended I try odesk as a first source of my new career. This would do until I got my first million pounds book deal at least!

I registered in March (approximately one month before I was due to leave my job) and applied for as many contracts as I could. I had no work between then and when I left my job at the end of April. In fact it took me until June to get my first contract! I was so relieved and was soon offered a second and then a third and the ratings started rolling in.

Everything Changes

It cannot be overstated that your life will change. You will become responsible for what you earn, your mistakes and your successes. It takes a special kind of person to be a freelancer. Drive and motivation is only the beginning; you have to fundamentally change everything you previously thought you knew about the working environment. The 9-5 is a thing of the past. You're going to get frantic messages from the other side of the world at 3AM like "I need this quickly!" You might relish the lie-in and working 10-6 or 11-7 but with no previous job have I woken up at 7am and begun work before my eyes have even opened properly.

I can't function without my morning coffee and I have two hours left to complete this urgent task that seems at least a five hour job! Weekends are also a thing of the past. I am in the UK and have a number of clients in Australia. By the time I wake up in the morning, they have usually left work for the day. Because of this, my typical working week is Sunday-Thursday. Most typically it is Sunday afternoon until Friday morning and during the week, I will typically work 10am until 7pm, sometimes later if I have a lot of work on and want to use a couple of hours to search for new work.

Making Mistakes is How We Learn

It's always great to get the email first thing in the morning that says "Exactly what I wanted – no changes, well done!" but nobody is perfect - we all make mistakes and once the work becomes a regular thing you will find clients who are never going to be happy with what you produce. Some will expect you to be a miracle worker and know what they want even when they themselves do not know. Some will be unhelpful and comment that as you are the writer, you should know what works. It cannot be stated enough that what will work for one client will not be suitable for the next.

Finding that balance, that correct style, is always a matter of trial and error. It toughens you up far more than any boss nagging in your ear! Take their comments on board and make the right changes, notice the tone and style that they are looking for because it might be very different to a similar job you completed last week

The Tricks SomeClients Try

After nearly a year of working through odesk, I have come up against a number of tricks that some potential clients use. Some of these I have learnt the hard way:

- Free samples: No matter how many verifiable links you post, or experiences you can cite, you will get requests for free samples. Most of these will be 100 words which you can produce in a matter of minutes, but some will ask for complete articles. Before you agree, check their status. Do they have a work history? Is their payment method verified? If the answer to both of these is "no" then the chances are that the job is not legitimate.

  I once had a contract that was fully verified but has asked myself and three others to complete the work before they would allocate the job. This, they stated, was so they could choose which one they liked and then pay the writer in retrospect. I politely declined

- Money Issues: Arguing about rates will come in many forms but the two most common for me is the client selecting that they are willing to pay "Expert Rates" (highest rates for the most experienced odeskers) but when the negotiations begin, the story changes. The second most common is the "I know someone who'll do it cheaper" – usually their regular writer who isn't available this week.

Both of these have happened to me. In the first instance, a client stated that their boss had initially authorised my $20ph but after agreeing to give me the contract, would I take $5ph instead? The second was for a contract I did actually work on in the end. The client claimed that my rate was the highest amongst his three writers but after two weeks he ended their contracts, leaving me the only team writer. I suspect that their poor level of English made him reconsider

- Number confusion:They'll want extra work and they won't want to pay for it because of their tight budget. Their boss initially wanted three articles but now they want a fourth for another website, but they can't afford to pay extra for it.This usually comes with the promise of more work in future but the promise of work is not a contract and you will sadly find yourself getting paid less for your professional service while waiting on repeat work that will never appearOdesk and sites like it are opening up the world for a truly global marketplace and connecting people with opportunities they might never have had before, or one that might have taken years to get a foothold. In less than a year, I have learnt about Australia's national strategy for making commercial buildings energy efficient, compared 7-seater cars for family suitability and learnt about disability employment law. I have to ask myself where else but odesk might I have been able to do that?

-Matthew Mason, United Kingdom-

2

ONLINE FREELANCING SITES

Best Websites for Freelance Jobs

Last updated: January 07, 2014

The outstanding new freelance jobs website <u>Freelancer</u> or <u>Elance</u> are the best choices among all the sites out there, if you want to hire someone or find projects to work online.

Hiring and working on these freelance websites is safer, easier and more profitable than finding anonymous people on the internet that you cannot trust. I don't say you cannot find honest people on the net, I'm just saying that it's way better to have a safe playground that is intermediated by a trustworthy third party site.

On these freelancing websites presented here, all transactions are mediated in a safe environment to assure fairness and transparency. You can stay relaxed that you will not lose money or time.

Below is the top 3 plus 4 mentions. They are the oldest, most trustworthy and reliable websites designed for micro-outsourcing and freelance jobs.

Top 7 Freelance Websites with Reviews

1. Freelancer - https://www.freelancer.com

The most visited freelance website in the World (453 global ranking according to Alexa) and the largest outsourcing marketplace.

Freelancer recently acquired one of the biggest player in the business, vWorker, after the acquisition of Scriptlance, making a huge expansion and creating almost a monopoly.

You can find a lot of projects at fair prices, but a relatively high competition.

It was started in 2003 and connects to more than 7 million employers and freelancers from all over the World.

- Disadvantages: There is a fee between 3 – 10% for freelancers. Minimum $30 per project.

+ Advantages: Free bidding for workers. Very fast & convenient to work on the platform.Accepts PayPal and Skrill.

[+] Read Freelancer Review.

2. Elance - https://www.elance.com/

If you want a world of talent on your fingertips, Elance is the best website to hang around.

Started in 1999, this babe is almost on the top of the list with over 90.000 jobs posted each month.

You can find web designers, developers, writers, Search Engine Optimization experts and anyone you need, from all over the world.

- Disadvantages: 8.75% fee. You must verify a PayPal account or a CC (Credit Card).

+ Advantages: Very User-friendly, High Quality workers & Escrow services.

[+] Read Elance Review

3. oDesk – https://www.odesk.com

The bronze medal is going to oDesk. Ranked 495 in Alexa Top, higher than Elance, oDesk is a very professional platform where a lot of successful businesses outsource their work.

They have cool features like sharing the desktop and verifying the time worked with visual time sheets. If you want a virtual assistant or you have an ongoing project, Odesk is the best choice in the matter.

- Disadvantages: You must verify you credit card.

+ Advantages: High quality. Super fast work.Small prices.

4. 99designs - https://99designs.com/

Here you post a design request and then a crowd of designers compete with each other for your prize. You then choose the best design, or you can reject all if you want. This is very good for outsourcing logo and graphic designs.

You can buy already made original & unique logos from a logo store.

If you want to receive multiple versions from as many people as possible, this is your choice for the best freelance website.

5. Guru – https://www.guru.com

This domain was first registered in 1988, but the website has a ten times smaller amount of traffic, compared with Freelancer.

Alexa Traffic Rank for Guru is 4,179, where Freelancer is at 434 at the top of the most visited websites in the World. So you will find fewer freelance workers and projects here.

6. Peopleperhour - http://www.peopleperhour.com/

This freelance website is ranked 4.201 in Alexa and it was started in 2007, so it's relatively new compared with top 3 websites.

7. Fiverr- http://www.fiverr.com

This is not an usual freelance website where you bid for projects, but rather a funny website where you can get people to do things only for five dollars. For example a project looks like "I will send 2500 twitter followers for $5". Cool… right?

This top seven is made after careful research, including personal experience, statistics and major trends in the business world.

More about freelance jobs

On these websites it's very easy to find freelance jobs or hire and delegate others to do the work for you. There are a lot of good options to search or post freelance work about a multitude of projects in:

Website Design, Graphic Design, Data Entry, Freelance Writing, SEO, Mobile Apps, Java, WordPress, PHP, Transcription, Translation and anything else, …

If you are a passionate freelancer or if you want to outsource online work, you should definitely check one or more of these websites.

Then, there is also the social media like Twitter, Facebook, forums and online chat rooms, but here you don't have any secure platform to be assured.

Land of the Freelancers, Home of the Brave: How to Find Your Next Freelance Gig Online

*By **Jenny An** — February 27, 2013*

So you want to work on a new project or just want to make some extra money and you're starting to think the freelancing life might be the one for you. Where to turn?

When you hop onto a popular site like oDesk, Freelance.com, Elance, and Guru, it's overwhelming. It can seem like all the jobs pay $5 an hour or less, and there are 50 other people who've already bid on the job with more logged hours than you.

And the competition for junk jobs where the clients want lengthy articles in "perfect English" at a pay rate of $1 per story aren't much better. So how do you avoid the programming jobs that want you to perfect a WordPress blog for a $10 flat rate?

The big clearinghouses for freelance writing and programming gigs feature thousands of jobs from around the world and also thousands of applicants. Rich Pearson, Chief Marketing Officer of Elance, says that 50 percent of their freelancers are full-time. However, many of those workers are based in countries where the cost of living is a lot lower.

All the primary sites offer promises of a payment guarantee – though the quality of escrow and payment dispute varies. Each service stresses the need for a full, typo-free profile with portfolio pieces and a full resume as the key to success. That sounds pretty simple, right?

Well, with over a million freelancers on each site, the competition can sometimes be brutal until you find a way to distinguish yourself on that stats-focused systems. A great resume and cover letter might get you the first job, but don't hold your breath for a full time gig ... at least, not a great one.

There are other options, and also how you can put in the elbow grease to make the big guys work for you:

The big dogs: oDesk, Guru, Freelance.com and Elance

Elance

Elance <u>shares its average hourly rates</u> for a plethora of specialties from French translation to C++ programming. Most are around $20 an hour or more, which certainly isn't a bad starting place. There are tests with the service so you can show off your coding skills – and yes, that is certainly a time investment, but it could end up saving you wasted moments on a dead end gig.

Pearson says that a third of freelancers get their jobs through invitations, not by applying directly to a post. This sounds great at first: Less time spent looking and more time getting paid!

But it also means having to work a lot of crappy projects to get your stats up so you appear in searches. "Once you have some success, you are shown to more [people hiring] due to our levels system

– this is a proprietary way of ranking our freelancers, based on earnings, timely project completion, skill tests taken and activity. As you achieve a higher level, you are presented to more clients and ranked higher on our freelancer search platform," Pearson says. Another pro tip: Pearson strongly recommends including all the keywords you're capable of (SEO writing on top of Search Engine Marketing) in order to be searchable.

oDesk

oDesk has a similar barrier to entry, requiring you to clock in some hours and receive some reviews first. Many clients hiring explicitly list needing at least one completed hour, and 100 hours isn't uncommon. And their payment guarantee system doesn't promise payment on fixed rate projects.

Guru

With a strangely similar interface to oDesk, Guru does pretty much the same as Elance and oDesk on a slightly smaller scale. It has received positive comparisons about its dispute and ratings systems compared to the big guns.

Freelance.com

Out of all the big companies, Freelancer.com is built on a model of cheap work for clients. It's homepage proclaims: "Only pay freelancers once you are happy with their work" and "Projects start at $30 and the average job is under $200⊠ which are nice to hear if you're hiring, but not quite as encouraging if you're looking for a job.

The job boards

<u>FlexJobs</u>

A massive bin of jobs which can be loosely interpreted as "flexible" (telecommuting, part-time, freelance, etc.), this service requires a subscription—pretty steep at $14.95 a month—for access to its troves of positions (in a board range of fields) and the ability to create a profile which allow you to be found. Their jobs are almost always legitimate companies but often can be found elsewhere for free with a little work.

<u>Freelance Switch</u>

Heavy on the programming and tech blogging realms, this is a job board that requires an account, costing you $7 per month to apply to positions.

ProBlogger

An extensive, easy to navigate job board for writers with mostly quality jobs ... and some not so appealing ones.

The niche markets

Contently

Targeted at writers, this site offers a gated sign-up which means that the quality is high—both for jobs and concerning the competition. Still in beta-mode, this is one place where experienced writers can do really show their stuff (success stories include a Boston Globe stringer who turned Contently into a $50,000 a year full-time job with time to write a book) but there aren't enough jobs for a newbie to push their way in.

"For entry- or mid-level freelance journalists, the best way to get noticed is to have great clips, stats, and logos next to your name. It's tough for a newbie to break in, but all it takes is one clip at The Wall Street Journal for the WSJ logo to show up at the top of your portfolio," says cofounder and Chief Creative Officer Shane Snow. However, job finding on the platform is in the hands of those doing the hiring – there's no way to apply, you really just have to get noticed, so get those clips in.

CrowdSpring

Taking crowd-sourcing to the design and branding realms, this is a great site if you're looking to build a design portfolio … not so much if you want to make money. Designs are submitted to each proposal and while payment for the design winner is guaranteed (and sometimes the runners-up get prizes too), with more than 100 entries on average for each project, competition is stiff.

CollabFinder

Another source of more inspiration than a paycheck, this site is great if you're looking to partner with someone on a project (mostly Internet startups). With success stories like <u>Makers Row</u>, a platform which allows designers to connect with American manufacturers that has gotten more than $75,000 in angel investing, there are plenty of great ideas floating around. However, the monetizing part is anything but guaranteed.

The first work of my life was for Odesk

"I'm 18 years old, I just finished high school last year and soon I will begin University. In my country to find a job when you are 18 is extremely difficult. All job searches ask for some kind of experience, and as very young people don't have experience, you are in an endless loop. No experience, no Job. No job, no experience. When I saw my dad working for Odesk, I thought there could be a job waiting for me there. So I began to look for my first job in Odesk.

First I quoted low rates, however there are people who quote ultra-low rates; and after all I do need to make money, so ultra-low rates were not an option ,at least in my situation. Then I realized there are people (or clients) looking for serious, honest and highly committed people. The internet it's not the easiest place to show to others how serious or honest you are. However it is possible, if you communicate very often, show interest in providing good results, doing a quality job and going an extra mile for clients, opportunities are there.

I found my first job on Odesk in less than one week."

-Juan B, Spain-

http://www.digitaltrends.com/social-media/finding-your-next-freelancing-gig-online/?tru=BXriB#comments

3

FREELANCE DESIGN PROJECTS

Tips for brand-new freelance designers

GUEST ARTICLE **by Nicole Foster –**

The switch to becoming a freelance designer is difficult because you have to learn how to handle yourself and your client. When I started out, I was completely clueless and I would often accept too many projects or bad clients. As I dealt with more clients and learned from other freelancers, I began to grow as a person and started to realize my mistakes. The first step to becoming a freelance designer is hard, but with the help of other freelancers, it is well worth it. Here are a few tips I picked up as a freelance designer that I wish I had known when just starting out.

Client Relations

Clients are the most important part of your freelancing career. Without them, you wouldn't have money or pieces in your portfolio. Knowing this, you need to be armed with a solid knowledge of client relations to keep getting clients and maintain the ones you have worked so hard to find.

- Don't undersell yourself to clients.
- Explain your process in simplest terms.
- Your client is not always right and it is okay to respectfully disagree.
- Having great customer service goes a long way.
- Always have the client deposit a certain percentage of the money up-front.
- If a client is angry with you, do not respond immediately to them; give yourself a few minutes to cool-off.
- Go the extra mile for your clients.
- Create a contract or terms and make your clients stick to it.
- Strive to get long-term clients and referrals.
- Always be professional.

When Designing

We all have different ways of approaching the design process. Some go straight to the computer and some start off with a pencil. Either way, it is important to remember certain aspects while you design. Here are a few of my tips:

- Always sketch out your ideas first before designing on the computer.
- Research your client's target audience before designing.
- Think of the user and NOT yourself while designing.
- Look for outside sources to inspire you instead of design galleries.

Time and Project Management

Time and project management are two keys to effectively freelance designing. You have to face the fact that you will receive multiple projects at one point. Once you have come across that, you need to make sure you are managing your time effectively and you are managing the project effectively or your project could collapse.

- Learn to "productively procrastinate"; which means you work on what is most important first.
- Don't make procrastination a habit.
- Find a project management application you like and stick to it.
- Frequently use a to-do list.
- Outsource to other designers when you are busy.

Marketing

Freelance designers often think they can bypass marketing, but you can't. To reach potential clients, you need to constantly market yourself and prove your worth over others. Here are a few marketing tips for new freelance designers:

- Create an effective elevator speech.

- Use social media to your advantage.
- Advertise yourself locally as well as globally.
- Create business cards and hand them out whenever you can.
- Never advertise your services on internet forums.
- Look for work on Job Boards.
- Research your target audience and find out where they go on the internet.

Some Other Important Things

Some of these tips are very important. Starting out, I wish I would have known most of these tips because they have severely hurt my business and hurt myself. Without realizing some of these tips, I would not be where I am today and I would not be as happy as I am today.

- Have a diversified portfolio.
- Get an email client for your desktop.
- Learn from your mistakes and move on.
- Do not accept every project you are offered.
- Learn from criticism instead of shrugging it off.
- Step away from your computer and get some sunlight.
- Exercise is important.

About Nicole Foster

 Nicole Foster is a professional website designer from New York that loves meeting new people. At Nicole Foster Designs, she offers website, wordpress, and ecommerce services to unique businesses. In her free time, she enjoys meditating and chatting with other designers.

http://www.graphicdesignblender.com/40-tips-for-brand-new-freelance-designers-2

20 Signs You Don't Want That Web Design Project

*Most clients are good clients, and some clients are great clients. But some jobs are just never going to work out well. Herewith, a few indicators that a project may be headed to the toilet. **Guarantee**: All incidents taken from life.*

1. Client asks who designed your website.
2. Client shows you around the factory, introducing you to all his employees. Then, behind closed doors, tells you: "If you do a bad job with this website, I'm going to have to let these people go."
3. Client takes six months to respond to your proposal, but doesn't change his due date.
4. At beginning of get-acquainted meeting, client informs you that someone has just bought his company.
5. Client, who manufactures Russian nesting dolls, demands to know how many Russian nesting doll sites you have designed.
6. At meeting to which you have traveled at your own expense, client informs you that he doesn't have a budget per se, but is open to "trading services."
7. Client can't articulate a single desired user goal. He also can't articulate a business strategy, an online strategy, a reason for the site's existence, or a goal or metric for

improving the website. In spite of all that, client has designed his own heavily detailed wireframes.

8. As get-acquainted meeting is about to wrap, the guy at the end of the table, who has been quiet for an hour and 55 minutes, suddenly opens his mouth.

9. Leaning forward intensely, client tells you he knows his current site "sucks" and admits quite frankly that he doesn't know what to do about it. He asks how you would approach such a problem. As you begin to speak, he starts flipping through messages on his Blackberry.

10. Client announces that he is a "vision guy," and will not be involved in the "minutia" of designing the website. He announces that his employee, the client contact, will be "fully empowered" to approve each deliverable.

11. On the eve of delivery, the previously uninvolved "vision guy" sends drawings of his idea of what the web layout should look like. These drawings have nothing to do with the user research you conducted, nor with the approved recommendations, nor with the approved wireframes, nor with the approved final design, nor with the approved final additional page layouts, nor with the approved HTML templates that you are now integrating into the CMS.

12. Your favorite client, for whom you have done fine work in the past, gets a new boss.

13. The client wants web 2.0 features but cannot articulate a business strategy or user goal.

14. Shortly before you ship, the company fires your client. An overwhelmed assistant takes the delivery. The new site never launches. Two years later, a new person in your old client's job emails you to invite you to redesign the site.

15. Client sends a 40-page RFP, including committee-approved flow diagrams created in Microsoft Art.

16. Client tells you he has conducted a usability study with his wife.

17. Client begins first meeting by making a big show of telling you that you are the expert. You are in charge, he says: he will defer to you in all things, because you understand the web and he does not. (Trust your uncle Jeffrey: this man will micromanage every hair on the project's head.)

18. As approved, stripped-down "social networking web application" site is about to ship, a previously uninvolved marketing guy starts telling you, your client, and your client's boss that the minimalist look "doesn't knock me out." A discussion of what the site's 18-year-old users want, backed by research, does not dent the determination of the 52-year-old marketing guy to demand a rethink of the approved design to be more appealing to his aesthetic sensibility.

19. While back-end work is finishing, client rethinks the architecture.

20. Client wants the best. Once you tell him what the best costs, he asks if you can scale back. You craft a scaled-back proposal, but, without disclosing a budget or even hinting at what might be viable for him, the client asks if you can scale it down further. After you've put 40 hours into back-and-forth negotiation, client asks if you can't design just the home page in Photoshop.

http://www.zeldman.com/2008/12/04/20-signs-you-dont-want-that-web-design-project/

10 DIFFERENT TYPES OF CLIENTS

December 2nd, 2008 - Posted by <u>Rebecca Kelley</u> to <u>Moz News</u>

The author's posts are entirely his or her own (excluding the unlikely event of hypnosis) and may not always reflect the views of Moz.

After having worked with a number of clients as well as listened to my colleages talk about companies and folks they've worked with, I thought I'd draft up a handy list identifying the various types of clients you may run into. I've found that this list is extremely official and scientific, so you should be able to refer to it and instantly identify a potential client. ;) Enjoy!

1. The Gabbo Client

The name for this client stems from the episode of The Simpsons titled "<u>Krusty Gets Kancelled</u>." In the episode everyone in Springfield sees commercials and billboards saying "Gabbo! Gabbo! Gab-bo!", but nobody knew what the heck Gabbo was. A Gabbo Client is someone who hires you to help out with their site, and when you take a look at the site you have no idea what the hell they're selling, what the site's purpose is, what it's focusing on, or why it even exists.

You: "What...is this?"

Client: "We've got videos!"

You: "Yeah...I'm still not getting it though. What's the site's purpose?"

Client: "Check out this funny article about marshmallows! We've got another one about Jay-Z!"

You: "Uh, so...you're selling...rap s'mores?"

You're gonna like me! You're gonna LOVE me!

2. The Lumbergh Client

You've all seen <u>Office Space</u>, so I'm sure you're familiar with the boss, Bill Lumbergh. A Lumbergh Client is someone who is unfazed by your efforts and instead needs you to "go ahead" and make a bunch of ridiculous changes to their site, even if you're only providing consulting work.

Client: "Yeeeeah, I'm gonna need you to go ahead and manage our paid search account."

You: "I don't do paid search."

Client: "Greeeeat. I'm also gonna need you to redo our landing pages and increase clickthrough rates by 110%."

You: "I'm only providing consulting. Don't you have a team or a staff to handle these--"

Client: "Greeeeeat. We'll touch base at the end of the week." [hangs up]

Yeeeeahhhh...

3. The Flatterbut Client

Flatterbuts are people who flatter you, then follow it up with a "...but..."

Client: "This site design is really incredible."

You: "Why thank you! I'm glad you like it!"

Client: "Really, this is just great work."

You: Aw, well thanks."

Client: "I just love it...buuuuuuut...I really want the whole thing to be in Flash."

You: "Again, I really appreciate your--wait, what?"

4. The Jessie Spano Client

For all you Saved By the Bell fans out there, I'm sure you remember the infamous episode where goody goody Jessie Spano gets addicted to caffeine pills and freaks out:

A Jessie Spano Client is someone who initially is "so excited" to work with you but ultimately gets overwhelmed by all the changes that you recommend and has a massive freakout from the stress of having to do a complete site overhaul. Most Jessie Spano Clients don't end up implementing any of your recommendations because they're afraid of a) losing rankings (even though you repeatedly tell them it's temporary at worst), b) confusing customers with the new "confusing" design, c) making the site more complicated, or d) all of the above.

5. The BTJ Client

The BTJ Client (or Bigger Than Jesus) is someone who is obsessed with getting a PR9 or PR10 site, no matter what you tell them or how hard you try to convince them that Page Rank isn't something they should obsess over.

Client: "I really want us to get a PR10 ranking."

You: "Um, for your wool socks site?"

Client: "Yes. It can't be that hard, right? Lots of sites have PR10s, yeah?"

You: "Well, there's Google.com..."

Client: "Okay, maybe a PR10 is a bit of a lofty goal. How about a PR9? I think we're PR9 material. Which sites have a PR9?"

You: "Uh, Yahoo.com..."

6. The DEFCON 1 Client

We've all had a DEFCON 1 Client. They somehow manage to freak out over *everything*.

Client: "Did you get my 24 emails?!"

You: "I saw them in my inbox and thought I'd call. Is something wrong?"

Client: "YES! It's terrible! I don't know what to do! How do we fix this?!"

You: "What's wrong?"

Client: "When I check my site's rankings from home it says we're at #5, but then when I'm at the office it says we're at #6!"

You: "Uh..."

Client: "Also, Yahoo! Site Explorer said we had 312,947 links last week, but this week it's only reporting 312,522 links! How'd we lose 400 links in a week?!"

You: "Oh dear..."

7. The H8tr Client
(aka The Haterade Client, aka The Negative Nelly Client)

You know how it goes with these guys:

You: "What did you think of my recommendations?"

Client: "Hated them. Can't execute any."

You: "Uh...well, what about our design mockups?"

Client: "Not one is remotely feasible."

You: "Well, did you at least get my holiday gift basket?"

Client: "I'm allergic to nuts. Also, I hate Christmas."

8. The T-800 Client

This quote from <u>The Terminator</u> sums up T-800 Clients quite nicely:

It can't be bargained with. It can't be reasoned with. It doesn't feel pity, or remorse, or fear. And it absolutely will not stop, ever, until you are dead.

Well, maybe not dead. More like "it will not stop until you've gotten it top rankings."

Client: "I want #1 rankings."

You: "Well actually it looks like you're getting great clickthrough and conversion rates from the position you're currently at, so I don't know how much moving up a couple spots will help you out..."

Client: "I want #1 rankings."

You: "I mean, if anything, you could focus on usability and worry more about the customer experience on your site..."

Client: "I want #1 rankings."

You: "Sigh. Okay, I'll see what I can do."

Client: "I'll be back."

Either looking for Sarah Conner or top rankings...

9. The Brainy Smurf Client

This type of client fancies himself an expert on Internet marketing despite actually knowing very little. He usually latches onto a buzz word he's just heard and spouts nonsensical information in a smug, know-it-all fashion:

Client: "We're really angling for a holistic social media approach, because, you know, content is king and we need that link juice!"

You: "What do you mean exactly?"

Client: "Well, you're supposed to be the expert, but I'll tell you what I think. Basically, we really think that canonical long tail latent semantic indexing is what's going to put our site over the top...blogosphere."

You: "Is that even English?"

Client: "Linkerati!"

Jerk.

10. The Holy Grail Client

Finding a Holy Grail Client is like finding a $20 bill in a six-month old Christmas card that you were going to throw away. It's like stepping on the scale and discovering you've lost 10 lbs. It's like trying something for the first time and discovering that you're a natural. While the perfect client isn't quite as elusive as unicorns, leprechauns, or unicorn-riding leprechauns, they're nonetheless tough to come by. Nonetheless, once you do work with a Holy Grail Client, you remember how satisfying client work can be. These are the folks who are excited to work with you, trust your recommendations, appreciate your hard work and efforts, understand your reasoning and are able to grasp various concepts, and genuinely love everything you've done for them. Holy Grail Clients make me happy.

I wish they were all like you...

What types of clients have I failed to mention? Got any good ones to share? Post your suggestion in the comments and I'll award the best one (don't thumb spam because I'm just going to pick the one that I like the best) a free month of SEOmoz PRO. Or, if you don't want PRO access, I can send you a can of Redbull or a lock of Rand's hair or something. We'll figure it out...

UPDATE: Congrats to Sprise for adding The Pusher to the list of clients. He wins the prize! Sprise, your lock of Redbull-soaked Rand hair is in the mail. ;)

About Rebecca — Rebecca Kelley is the content marketing manager for Intego, a Mac software company. She also guest-blogs/freelances at various places and runs a couple hobby blogs for shits and giggles.

<u>Sean Roach</u>

The Pusher is so named because of (1) their unnecessarily strict deadline push, (2) your need for the caffeine pusher to meet said deadline, and (3) your need to find a real pusher for chemical remedy after dealing with this type of client. The interaction goes something like...

- o Mon - you: "We can have this done next Friday" / client: «I need it this Friday» / you: «We›ll see what we can do.
- o Tue - client: "Friday, right?" / you: "See what we can do."
- o Wed - client: "Friday, right?" / you: "Not looking good, but we'll see what we can do."
- o Thu - client: "Friday, right?" / you: "We'll get it done."
- o Fri - you [after three consecutive all-nighters]: "Here it is!"
- o Weekend - *nothing*
- o Mon - *nothing*
- o Tue - *nothing*
- o Wed - you: "Any feedback?"
- o Thu - *nothing*
- o Fri - client: "Haven't had a chance to review yet, but will sometime next week.

<u>http://moz.com/blog/10-different-types-of-clients</u>

My oDesk Story as a Freelance Graphic Designer

The year after I had graduated college from CSUN with a BFA in Graphic Design, I was waiting tables and perpetually grating cheese at a little known restaurant called The Cheesecake Factory. I also was having a horrible time getting into a Design or Advertising Firm due to the competition of my field and the location of where I lived. Los Angeles, being a true Mecca of Art and Design, seems like an easy place to get a job but honestly it is a dense sprawl making it hard to get around town, often overwhelmingly crowded, and extremely superficial. Feeling defeated and very poor, I consoled in a friend and she told me about oDesk and other Online Freelance Websites. I was interested but didn't really know the perks of this life changing technology. I signed up and started working immediately designing logos, professional pamphlets, and posters. I was earning very little at first but for the most part I had amazing clients from ALL OVER THE WORLD! I eventually got up to the pay grade I desired as my portfolio grew. There were only a few people that tried to scam me into designing something for free over a fixed price but I figured there has to be a few bad apples.

My most favorable and memorable experience was designing an "Open Mic" Poster for a Charity event. The gentleman I worked with was a member of the Church and wanted to have a flyer for his event to promote fun and raise money for children in the Philippians. It was the first time I was able to design for a good cause and I will never forget how good it made me feel. oDesk is a big part of my success as a graphic designer and my individual happiness. Thank you oDesk and thank you World.

My worst experience was when I first started out and I was asked to design an advertisement for an online company that sold gaming products. I had created many variations of the ad and most importantly had prior to designing, asked him if he had the clearance to use such Company ownedimages, in which he confirmed he had. After spending many hours and correspondence, I found out he had no rights to use the Gaming Products, so I had omit my designs and did was not paid. C'est la vie.

-Anonymous, USA-

4

FREELANCE WRITING

9 Online Gold Mines for Finding Paid Freelance Writing Jobs

September 23, 2013 By Kelly Gurnett

Share on facebookShare on twitterShare on emailShare on pinterest_shareMore Sharing Services**151**

If you're a freelance writer, the task of finding quality, well-paying gigscan be a daunting one. Where do you even start? How you can guarantee the jobs you're looking at are legit instead of scams?

Let's get the bad news out of the way first: the Internet is chock full ofpeople who are willing to pay pennies on the dollar for hours of your highly skilled time. (Keep reading for some words of warning about these people.)

The good news is that we're here to help you weed out the dreck and find the sites that are actually worth your time and effort. (Click to tweet this list.) Whether you're a copywriter, editor, creative writer or anything in between, these sites offer the well-paying, reputable jobs you really want.

Better yet? While some sites charge a monthly fee to access their job listings, all of the resources below are free.

So where can you find freelance gigs?

BloggingPro Job Board: Also listing a healthy dose of copywriting jobs (you can search postings by category), this board is, as the name suggests, right up a blogger's alley. Whether you're into health and fitness, pets, writing code or what have you, you'll find a steady stream of employers looking for blog writers versed in these and many other subjects.

Freelance Writing Gigs: While anything on Craigslist should be taken with a grain of salt, this site does increase your chances of finding a decent gig by consolidating writing job posts from Craigslist boards all across the country, allowing you to locate telecommuting gigs you might never see if you were only browsing your local board. That said, Craigslist is still Craigslist. This site tries to exclude any posts that look like scams, but the onus is still on you to vet each listing carefully.

Journalism Jobs: While most of the postings are (you guessed it again!) for those interested in journalism jobs, you don't necessarily have to have Lois Lane dreams to find a gig here. There are also editing positions, ad copywriting and other jobs thrown into the mix. Some are location-based, some can be done remotely.

LinkedIn Jobs: If you've already got a LinkedIn profile (and you really should), don't just let it sit there. Networking goes a long way in the freelance world, and LinkedIn is a great resource to do some networking through common connections.

While you're doing that networking, check out the Jobs section and sign up for email alerts when jobs are posted that match your interests. Many will be location-based, but who's to say you can't approach these employers with a proposal for freelance services? Maybe they need someone to fill the gap in the hiring interim, or maybe the job could just as easily be done remotely but they hadn't considered that.

Pro tip: You know that "people who've recently viewed your profile" notification you see when you sign into LinkedIn? If you don't recognize some of the names, why not reach out to them and say "I see you've looked at my profile. I'd love to explore if there are any ways we can help each other." Can't hurt to try, right?

MediaBistro: Check out the freelance section of the site for a wide range of jobs from industries like TV, PR/marketing, magazine and book publishing and social media–a little something for everyone.

Morning Coffee Newsletter: This weekly e-newsletter provides a nice compendium of freelance writing and editing jobs of all shapes and sizes from around the Web with competitive pay rates. Save yourself the time of scouring numerous sites and let this newsletter bring the decent jobs right to your inbox.

ProBlogger Job Board: From Darren Rowse of ProBlogger, an authority site on blogging, you know jobs listed here are going to be from serious employers who have an idea what good writing is really worth. Plus, given ProBlogger's high profile in the blogosphere, you can often find jobs posted by some big-time blogs here.

The Ultimate List of Better-Paid Blogging Gigs: Freelance blogger Sophie Lizard has compiled a free ebook listing 45 blogs that pay $50 or more per post, broken down into sections like Writing Blogs, Food Blogs, etc. She also includes some good tips on how to approach these blogs, how to promote yourself once you've landed a post, and more.

50 Markets That Pay Freelance Writers 10 Cents Per Word: Okay, so this ebook isn't free, but it's only $4.99, and if you land even one 500-word project, it will have paid for itself several times over. This book offers a compilation of contact information and guidelines for 50 magazines, newspapers, websites and ezines

that accept freelance pieces, so whatever your specialty, you're bound to find something that appeals to you.

Sites to avoid

Especially if you're just starting out, it's tempting to be lured into content mills like Demand Studios or free-for-alls like Guru, oDesk and Elance, where it looks like you might stand a better chance to land something even if you don't have the biggest portfolio yet.

Don't be.

While it may seem like these sites are your best best when you're a newcomer, they're largely a crapshoot when it comes to winning a project. These sites are a rush for the lowest bid, and you're competing against hundreds if not thousands of other desperate freelancers prepared to sell their firstborn for the chance to write someone's 250-page ebook.

Even if you're brand-spanking new to the game, no one deserves a gig that pays one cent per word. And chances are if someone is looking for the sort of writer willing to write a word a cent, they're not going to be the best client to work for. Don't sell yourself short just because you're new. Have a little patience, keep persevering, and you *will* find those clients who truly value you.

http://thewritelife.com/find-freelance-writing-jobs/

How to Become an Online Freelance Writer

Edited by S Swati, Luv_sarah, Krystle, Wingrider and 3 others

There are many struggles you may face to establish yourself as an online freelance writer. This article is here to help people and make their struggle a little more easy. So here goes...

Steps

1

Rediscover your passion for writing. A profession like online writing is definitely for someone who has had a flair for writing. Maybe a small poem for the school magazine , a short essay for the college daily- the love for penning down thoughts in a manner that appeals to others...is the only criteria required. There will come a point in life, when every other thing around you becomes mundane enough or you want that extra little income. Freelance writing is just the option for you!

2

Experiment with your friends & family: Friends & family can help you, be at your side when you need them most. This is the time. Make them go through, in some degree of detail, the very first thoughts that springs from your mind onto paper (or a word doc). More importantly so, if you are writing after long years of inaction. And yes, listen to every feedback they give you. They are your first readers, after all.

3

Don't get too carried away with their comments: Most family members will tell you is that your article is good. But make sure, they do not score a 10/10 for an article written badly. Ask them to give you a frank opinion or an objective view, no matter how bad that might sound to you. This will ensure that the world outside doesn't come back to you with harsher comments or you are able to take the discouragement that might be associated with your first (few)publications.

4

Write more than 5 articles in the beginning: A good writer is most essentially a prolific one. The easiest way to give a good launch to your freelance writing career is to write a lot. Review the book that you read lately or a movie you liked. You can write about job hassles, misadventures with your boss or colleagues, a relaxed evening spent with your sweetheart or a good date that you had lately. If you have kids, you will never run out of topics to write about!

5

Articles should represent your point of view and not you.
Writing an article about yourself (or others) should not sound like a private opinion. Remember, there is a difference between writing your personal diary and writing an article about yourself. Be personal but draw a line, where it is required. Similarly, if you are writing about a particular topic or a social issue, make sure there are some facts in there (Google/Wikipedia provide you with loads of them) and not just your associated thoughts.

6

Start a Blog: Blogs are in! They are free (literally) for you to play around, go wild with your thoughts and post whatever you like. But again be careful that whatever you are posting will be read by editors with whom you may apply a future freelance job. So act accordingly. Project that part of you that can make your career as a successful freelance writer. This blog should be your forte, your strength, the expression of your freedom.

7

Practice sitting for hours with your laptop. If you are a home maker, finish the laundry, the dishes, the cooking, get plenty of cushions and go! This is definitely going to take time and needs peace & quiet! When a train of thoughts start flowing, it is wise to convert them to words immediately lest they be forgotten within the next few minutes. A beautiful word, a funny line, a thought-provoking quote... generally don't come back to you by the time you grab that cookie from kitchen or have a quick chat with your next door neighbor.

8

Speed up office assignments. Office goers who are planning to freelance have a tough job to do as well. Balancing work, home and writing is definitely a challenge. Its still easy if you work in shifts, but a regular 9 to 6 job requires either late nights or early morning sacrifices to be made. Plus it also depends on whether you are a morning person or a nocturnal one! This job requires hours and you should do whatever possible to give it a good, smart start.

9

Don't get discouraged by online scams. You will read about scores of scams, negative feedback, bad experiences etc. that people share, regarding their experience as online/print freelance writers. If you are starting your career as one, you also shall have your own share of sour sagas to narrate after some time. But don't let that clip the wings of your newly happening writing career. Always remember that tenacity and perseverance pay (literally!)

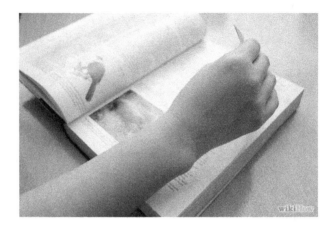

10

Research researchresearch. Yes, you just have to do plenty of it. Research on the web for all the agencies that give offer paid freelancing jobs. Make sure these sites are legitimate. Online user reviews will also give you a lot of information. Google, Bing or any other popular search engines might give you plenty of attractive ads but it is up to you to choose whether the agencies are authentic enough. Preferably, go for those people who offer an income (there are others to whom you have to pay for getting offers/jobs). In the end, bookmark the important sites and check if others have bookmarked them too.

11

Spend at least half a day per selected agency. Once you have shortlisted the agencies for whom your are going to contribute articles, research some more on them. Read reviews, published articles, testimonials, photographs of any meetings or camps they had in the past. The form you fill to subscribe to this agency should have proper online security checks. Don't give your email Id out randomly (the barge of spam will be too much to handle; plus there are added online security risks). Tread carefully and start by choosing just one, highly reliable web agency.

12

Write a pleasant article. Your first article should impress. The editors of the online agency will have tons of articles to skim through. Make their job easy & the freelancing job is yours! Your article should be precise, light (flowery or eloquent speeches are most unwelcome), slightly humorous and attention grabbing. Check out for spell, formatting & grammatical errors. The editors should be able to picture the reader enjoying this article & giving them a thumbs up.

13

Don't demand or expect an astronomical pay. Some freelance agencies that will ask you your expectations. Don't stretch out to your limits & name an amount that will repel them. Be modest and give ask for a moderate pay. Prices differ across agencies, jobs, countries and also the experience level of writers. As you are new, chances are that you are not quite known in the industry and will be paid accordingly. Most importantly, don't fall for websites that offer you that six-figure pay. The generally end up duping you royally.

14

Submit the article but don't give up. After submitting the article, keep your expectations low.If you are in luck and the agency selection is good, you have a fair chance of getting the amount that has been promised to you. But in case you don't get a dime, don't be disheartened. There are plenty of other opportunities. Try sending the articles to other online agencies or publications and keep the persistence up. If your work is good, you will surely be noticed & get the kind of work you want.

http://www.wikihow.com/Become-an-Online-Freelance-Writer

11 Websites to Find Freelance Writing Jobs

.Ever wondered how <u>freelance writers</u> find markets for their writing talent and the ability to write online articles too? Or where you could offer articles / blogs with a link to your book's sales page – as described in a former blog post: <u>Smart Authors Get Paid for Marketing Their Books</u>

Don't look further than to these websites, which are regularly updated, either on a weekly basis, and sometimes even more often. These links will lead you not only to get the latest job openings, but also great sources of publishing and writing knowledge:

http://www.writingjobsource.com

Writing Job Source connects writers with employers in one central place. They email writers every other day the latest offers.

http://www.absolutewrite.com

This site consist of valuable content, including some international market listings. Funny to read their FTC compliance…

http://www.duotrope.com

Their Motto: Write. Re-write. Submit. This free database contains more than two thousand writer markets for short fiction, poetry and novels/collections. Try out their custom searches of thousands of market listings to find exactly what you are looking for!

http://www.fundsforwriters.com

Author C. Hope Clark writes since many years a great weekly blog on freelance writing, writing jobs (full-time), grants, markets, contests and fellowships. Sign up for her free e-newsletter – you will be glad that you did. It is one of the very few newsletters that are truly worth subscribing!

http://www.fwointl.com

Freelance Writing Organization Intl. is a free online database with thousands of job listings and freelance opportunities. Over 5000 Free Writing Resources & Links, thousands of Writing Jobs Opportunities.

http://www.journalismjobs.com

Daily job listings for journalists, editors, online media and more.

http://www.marketlist.com

This database of markets and contests is helping freelance writers for over ten years.

http://www.mediabistro.com

Every freelancer should bookmark this site and visit often for the latest industry news and the great job listing section.

http://www.mediajobsearchcanada.com

"Job Search & Find" site for Canadian writers, journalists, editors, marketing & PR-specialists and radio or TV personnel.

http://www.mediajobmarket.com

Media Job Market lists hundreds of job postings and several fantastic must-read articles on job hunting in the writing industry.

http://www.writergazette.com

Writer Gazette's regularly weekly newsletter, forum, writer service listing and most important of all: More than 500 submission calls to paying markets.

http://jobs.problogger.net/

The ProBlogger Job Board is where professional bloggers looking for jobs and companies looking for bloggers to hire.

Essentials are: Learn to write for the web, know how to write press releases, and study potential contract givers' websites thoroughly. Update your portfolio regularly, and don't forget: the decision makers can also be found on social media sites, such as Google+ or Twitter. Keep your author appearance on Social Media professional, and post regularly links to the best of your writing. Being familiar with you and your writing can for sure improve your chances of getting more assignments.

http://savvybookwriters.wordpress.com/2013/08/24/9-websites-to-find-freelance-writing-jobs/

19 Online Communities to Find Freelance Writing Jobs

August 5, 2011 by <u>Alex Mathers</u>

There are many opportunities right now to earn money doing freelancing writing jobs, if anything to supplement the freelance work you are doing at the moment. I know how hard it is right at this moment to get regular clients and regular income, but if you have a knack with writing, you could make some nice earnings to fill in any gaps.

The great thing about working as a writer is that you can do it at a time that suits you, so that it complements anything else you are working on. There is currently a big need for quality written content, especially on the web, and you can take advantage of that need.

A fruitful place to find writing jobs that can provide some extra (or a lot) cash is online freelance job communities.

I've listed 19 good places that you can use to find the jobs that work for you:

Freelancewritinggigs.com

This site is a compilation of blogs, some of which post job leads.

Problogger.net

A site geared towards job postings for bloggers.

Poewar.com

Navigate through to the freelance writing jobs, where you will find jobs compiled from many sources in one easy to view screen.

Bloggerjobs.biz

Another site with a large listing of freelance blogging jobs.

Mediabistro.com

Narrow your search on this job listing site by checking "freelance" to obtain only the listings that are freelance based.

Freelanceswitch.com

This site includes a large listing of freelance writing job posting.

Sunoasis.com

Sunoasis provides links to a large volume of freelance writing opportunities compiled from many sources.

Journalismjobs.com

Under "Opportunities", narrow your search down to just freelance writing jobs. There are plenty of opportunities on this site to view.

Allfreelancewritingjobs.com

This blog provides weekly links to several job leads. You can also view previously posted jobs and apply to those as well.

Wahm.com

This work at home forum lists many job openings; search through the listings to find those for freelance writers.

Online-writing-jobs.com

This site also offers freelance writing job listings.

Sologig.com

Under "Browse by Categories" select "creative", and you will find a few writing jobs, and many freelance copywriting jobs.

Gofreelance.com

Go Freelance allows you to search by category. Sselect "writing" and view listing for freelance writing.

Freelancefree.com

A free site to register and find freelance work.

Freelancewriting.com

This is a comprehensive site that also lists freelance writing opportunities.

Indeed.com

At Indeed.com, search for "freelance" and you will find a multitude of freelance writing opportunities.

Virtualvocations.com

Virtual Vocations lists projects available for freelance writers.

Lancepost.com

Lancepost lists a feed of new job leads, sift through to find leads for freelance writing.

Worldwidefreelance.com

Through this site, check out the heading titled "markets". You can view their free leads and guidelines and also sign up for a newsletter.

Please do comment on your results from these sites, and if you know of others!

About the Author: Alex Mathers

Alex is a project starter, sometimes finisher, writer and illustrator. He started Red Lemon Club in 2009 with the aim of helping talented creative people leave their mark.

http://www.redlemonclub.com/resources/19-online-communities-to-find-freelance-writing-jobs/

Companies Offering Online Writing Jobs for Beginners

Kristina Choi, Yahoo Contributor Network Jun 3, 2010

The occupational outlook for freelance writers is very promising. However, like anything else, you must find a way to break into the freelance writing world. This can be difficult when you're just starting out, since you don't have much of a portfolio. To counteract this problem, you need to find companies offering entry-level writing jobs. Textbroker, The Content Authority and Internet Research Associates are three popular examples, as they are constantly offering online writing jobs for beginners. To find out more about each company, check out the sections below.

1. Textbroker

Textbroker is the first place you should go when investigating online writing jobs for beginners. Why? Well, first off, they don't necessarily pay you at a beginner's rate. If you do well on their sample test, it is possible that you could work at a Level 4. At this level, you will receive 1.4 cents per word, (as stated on the Textbroker website). This means a typical 400-word assignment would net you $6.30.

Assignment turnaround is another reason why Textbroker is the best choice for the beginning writer. From my experience, you have between 24 hours and six days to complete an assignment. If you cannot complete the assignment within the designated timeframe, you are not penalized in any way. You can even claim the assignment again, after it is deleted from your queue.

Finally, when it comes to online writing jobs for beginners, Textbroker is one company that will never run out of work. When I log into my account on any given day, I see thousands of articles available. In addition, if you can't find something decent on your level, you're always free to choose an assignment on a lower level.

2. The Content Authority

The Content Authority is another great place offering online writing jobs for beginners. And, like Textbroker, you can move up the different tiers they offer. However, there is a slight downside. When you are first hired with the company, you are put on a probationary period. During this time, you are placed on their lowest writing tier. According to their *New Writer's Orientation*, to get off of this level, you must submit 5 articles. From there, you will either stay at the beginner's level or get upgraded to the higher ones.

What happens if you don't get upgraded? Well, based on my time there I have found that even Tier 1 articles are lucrative, as I have received $2.10 per 300-word article. Multiply this by 5, and you make $10.50 per hour.

You can make even more money during the company's weekly contests. Used to help boost writer momentum, these contests grant money to writers that can complete the greatest number of Tier 1 articles. It doesn't even matter if you're on a higher tier, since Tier 1 articles are available to everyone.

Just keep in mind that all articles have an 8-hour turnaround time, another fact addressed in TCA's *New Writer's Orientation*. Failure to complete the article in this timeframe forfeits any compensation you might have made, as the assignment is released to another writer.

3. Internet Research Associates

Lastly, there is Internet Research Associates, one of the first companies I've seen to offer online writing jobs for beginners. How do they work? My experience has shown that you get paid $5 per 300-to-500 word article. Turnaround times vary depending on the client. Most of the assignments I've taken require a 3-day turnaround, though if you get an e-book you might be given up to a week. Either way, you must make sure that you can complete the assignment within the designated timeframe, since there are usually no extensions.

As far as the work itself, you are usually given the articles in batches, allowing for a higher payout. There are also opportunities to get more exclusive assignments, such as press releases or book reviews. Ultimately, if you are a good writer who can turn their work in on time, there are a plethora of opportunities Internet Research Associates has available for you.

Sources:

1. "<u>Author Payment</u>." Textbroker.

2. "<u>New Writer's Orientation</u>." The Content Authority. (Only Viewable to Authors)

<u>DISCLOSURE OF MATERIAL CONNECTION</u>:

The Contributor has a direct relationship to the brand or product described in this content.

<u>http://voices.yahoo.com/companies-offering-online-writing-jobs-beginners-6099144.html?cat=31</u>

NEVER TOO OLD TO CHANGE YOUR LIFE...

I began writing for oDesk last August. I had worked five years as a teacher in a small private school. I am fairly outspoken, especially when it comes to dealing with bratty seventh and eighth graders. A few parents complained, and they did not offer me a contract to return. That was all right with me – at sixty-six, I was ready to try something new.

My husband found information on-line about making money freelancing. He also downloaded Rory Parker's Writerpreneur, which answered many of the questions running through my head. Parker told of getting to a point where she needed to turn away jobs and could support herself full-time. She mentioned oDesk as being the easiest site for her to work with because it met her needs. I tried other sites, but many want you to "bid" – makes me feel like I am on the auction block. Also, I like the ease of use, layout, and payment policy at oDesk.

At first things went very slowly. I made some mistakes; I took the wrong jobs, got scammed, and did not charge enough. Fortunately, we were not dependent on my income. Parker mentioned in her book that it takes about three months to get started. She was right. I started at $10 an hour and now make $20.

However, I have discovered I prefer to write by the article or assignment. That way I can take as much time as I want and really produce a great article. Also, I sometimes forget to turn the clock on or off and get the time all messed up – remember I'm "age-impaired."

I can truly say that oDesk has changed my life. I have made new friends, learned new skills, and grown as a writer and a person. Probably my favorite thing about oDesk is that I have "friends" from all over the world. I have worked for Australians, Indians, Europeans, Canadians, South Americans, Middle Easterners and people from all over the United States.

My very first client, from Australia, is still requesting work from me monthly. My second client, from Pakistan, gave me valuable advice on how to choose jobs, meet my client's expectations, and told me about working flat-rate jobs.

When my daughter had a nervous breakdown, I was delayed with some assignments. All my clients were tremendously understanding and supportive. One, a retired U.S. military man in Hawaii with a homemade bread site (I wrote recipe introductions for him) was especially encouraging. His daughter had the same problem and he gave me a great deal of much needed advice and encouragement.

Last time I visited my daughter in Texas, I met a client for lunch. She is about my age and although our backgrounds, personalities, and interests are very different, we continue to communicate long after I completed her e-book. I plan to see her next time I visit Texas.

Maybe part of my intensive involvement with my clients is that I choose jobs that I believe "add value." I like to find jobs that will affect somebody or something in some positive way – provide information, helpwith or correct a problem, or cause individual growth. In addition, I look for on-going clients. Sometimes I take a job that does not pay as much as usual for the experience or to provide someone needed assistance.

Another aspect of oDesk is the opportunity to learn and grow. I firmly believe that we start to age when we stop learning and growing. I have researched and written on many different subjects – among them explainer videos, camel's milk, osteoarthritis of the spine, water speakers, earthquake preparedness, and yoga clothing.

I want to be an author.I am definitely a better writer due to freelance writing. I have been working on my first novel for years – yes, I am a perfectionist. My writing has improved due to the necessity of counting words and making each word count. The writing of product descriptions has improved my descriptive writing. I am starting back through my novel, and this time it will be ready for publication, as an e-book (since I now know all about those).

I have reached the conclusion that the greatest force for uniting the human race is the internet – specifically cross-cultural communication. Probably, the most important aspect of oDesk is its ability to break down barriers. I have learned that as humans we have a tremendous amount in common.

Political, racial, cultural, and religious lines disappear. Odesk has the power to change an individual's life and the world in which we live. It has definitely changed mine.

-Susan Mann, USA-

5

FREELANCE COMPUTING/ TECH JOBS

50 Freelance Job Sites For Designers & Programmers – Best Of

By **Dainis**. Filed in **Web 2.0**

Being a freelancer can be extremely advantageous and it is probably a dream for many designersand developers. Not only you get to choose the job you are really interested in, you also have total flexibility in terms of time, whom you want to work with and where you want to work at.

However, there is always a flip side of a coin. *What happens when if you are out of jobs suddenly?* This following article is dedicated to designers and developers who wanted to achieve financial freedom in freelancing. We showcase a list of **50 Best Freelance Job Sites** and you might want to go through to see if you've missed some of them. If you a company or individual looking to outsourcing or hire, these following sites might come in handy too. Full list after jump.

GetAFreelancer

Bag a project or post a project on this platform to get the best bids from gamut of skilled web designers, copywriters or freelance programmers. Provide work or get work at the best prices. Sign up today as a work provider or a work seeker. A word of caution – Stay alert before trusting anyone as there are a lot many fraudsters as well, on both sides.

Odesk

Since its inception in 2004, this online marketplace truly embarked a revolution in the way world works. It's win-win approach for both service providers and employers with meaningful work as well as top-flight talent, makes it an asset for both parties. Average size of a job here is $5,000.

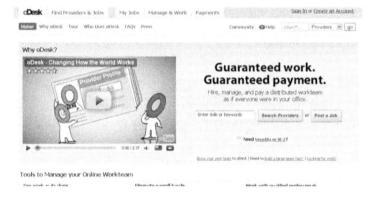

RentACoder

Rent a coder is a website where a software developer can get plenty of jobs there and in return can earn plenty of money. This is perfectly a legit site and the fact that it is only a medium for giving work to interested hunters makes it tempting.

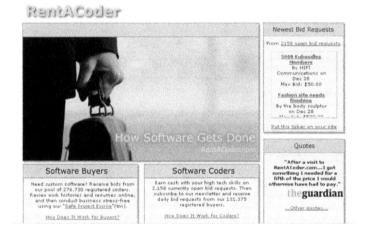

Project4hire

This freelance marketplace offers an array of opportunities to contractors and thereby require them to pay a small amount as a commission to tech site, on being awarded a project. Apart from this, it is easy to use and a great platform to post projects and find freelance professionals like coders, consultants, <u>graphic designers</u>, software developers.

Scriptlance

Get access to thousands of designers and programmers with immense in-depth knowledge about an array of programming languages, ranging from Joomla, C++ to SEO requirements.

GetACoder

The growth of a business is decided by the resources that it is able to explore and access, to get the competitive advantage. Save costs and enhance <u>efficiencies</u> by outsourcing your programming, writing and web designing jobs to the right people at this famous online freelance portal.

GetACoder.com

Home | My Account | Post Job | Browse Jobs | RSS Feeds |New!

Fast & Simple Job Outsourcing

Find Freelance Programmers, Web Designers and Freelance Writers for your next request. Outsource jobs to your home country or to countries where labor is cheap. Post a request for free and start receiving bids within minutes. Thousands of outsourced jobs prove that GetACoder is a cost-effective way to get the best talent in the world at an amazing low price. Grow your business and achieve a greater return on investment by using GetACoder. Post Your Job for FREE!

Web Design / Development (1887)
Database Development (710)
Writing (382)
Computer Platforms (158)
Engineering (75)
Testing / Quality Assurance (92)
Project Management (16)
Enterprise Resource Planning (81)
Training (49)

Programming (3240)
Graphics / Multimedia (329)
Marketing / Promotion (280)
Gaming (118)
Security (62)
Administrative Support (101)
Requirements (92)
Legal (29)

Software Buyers
Skilled and cost-effective freelance programmers, web designers and freelance writers are waiting to bid on your next request! Find out who people outsource jobs with us day after day. Registration is free & fast. more info

Digitalpoint Forum

Aside from being a very useful forum for webmaster, Digitalpoint is also an extremely strategic place where you can outsource work and seek relevant freelance professionals.

Smashing Jobs

A great thing about posting your job at this site is that the jobs
listed here are soon featured among one of the top 20 blogs of
the world. This is again a nice job portal to find programming
and designing jobs, besides all others.

Elance

A famous online portal for freelancers, this is an ultimate place to meet professionals with business, technical and marketing expertise to get work done at an affordable price.

Sitepoint Marketplace

Sitepoint is a well-known paid webmaster forum. Looking to hire category providers a marketplace where you can find freelancers or clients from different industries and different countries.

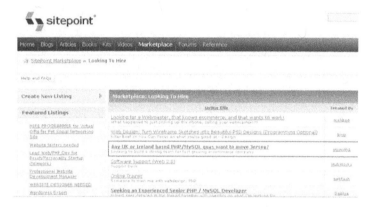

Simply Hired

This online job portal allows you to find all kinds of jobs, whether freelance or full-time, based on your location, skills and experience in the field.

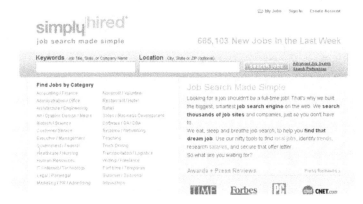

Metafilter Jobs

Search and share jobs with other members of the site and mark the distance of your job from you, based on the latitude/latitude entered in your profile.

December 15

Drywall magician (freyada)
posted to: soft and hardcore taters to skilled trades/artisan at 2:44 PM   details

Problogger Jobs

If you are also one of the blogging enthusiasts, who has or who wishes to explore the income potential of this fun-filled hobby of 'blogging,' problogger.net is your right choice. Collaborate with other bloggers, share experiences and take your blogs to great heights. The jobs section of this blog can land you with several blogging jobs that pays you well along with enjoying what you love to do.

Dice

Dice is a job search engine dedicated to only finding technology jobs. It offers a targeted niche space for finding exactly the technology position you might be looking for. Dice also offers advice on writing resumes and obtaining IT certification, as well as a variety of discussion forums.

Guru

Like other freelance websites, this is another of the sources to find the indutry's most ultimate professionals from world over. However, safer way to pay through Escrow gives this site an edge over other freelance sites. From business, creative arts to technology, select your favorite category and get started.

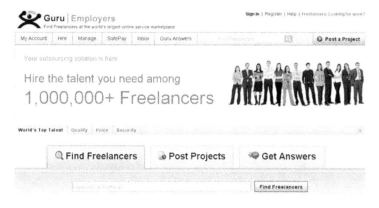

99designs

If you like to draw and your drawings are good and you want to earn from it, you can try your hand at 99Designs. 99Designs, basically is a site where various companies fulfill their need of designing their logos, banners, websites etc. They just give you the information about the background of their company, its ideas and goals. The designers use these facts and design logos or whatever is required by the company. If the contest holding company likes the job, it awards the designer with the pre specified prize money.

3. choose the best design!

Behance Job

Find productivity and creativity go hand in hand at the job list section of this site that claims to 'make ideas happen.' This exclusive site is known to convert creativity into lucrative services or products to promote unique ideas.

Mistersoft Freelancing

Your needs may encompass a flash <u>designer</u>, a copywriter, a SEO manager, a coder, a data entry expert or any other professional, find the best of the lot at this amazing site for freelancers.

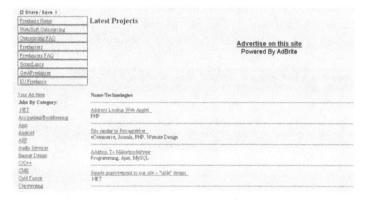

37signals Jobs

37signals job board provides a wide array of content from many geographies. If you're looking to hire programmers and designers from around the U.S., 37signals looks like a site worth dipping your feet into.

37signals Job Board now with internships too!   37signals

Industry leaders such as Apple, The New York Times, CNET, Facebook, Adobe, Trek, and American Express use this Job Board to reach today's best and brightest web minds. Discover why this job board will find you better people than other job sites.

Live search   Post a job (or internship) and find the right person
_____   Jobs are $300 for 30 days, internships are $50 for 30 days
| |

Show: ☑ Full-time Jobs ☐ Paid Internships

DESIGN JOBS LATEST POSTINGS FIRST   RSS FEED

San Diego, CA: Web Developer at MindTouch, Inc.

Mountain View, CA: Graphic Designer, Interactive Media at Geeknet, Inc.

Ottawa, Canada: Senior Web Designer at TravelPod (A TripAdvisor/Expedia Company)

Austin, TX: Senior UX Designer at BuildASign.com

Orlando, FL: Developer, Sr. Developer (DOE) at FOIU Business Exchange, Inc.

Houston, TX: PHP Web Application Developer at CPAP.com

Bixee

This hybrid job portal also form a part of Ibibo, which is a famous Indian social networking platform. Hence, you can find suitable jobs and research innovative content at the same time.

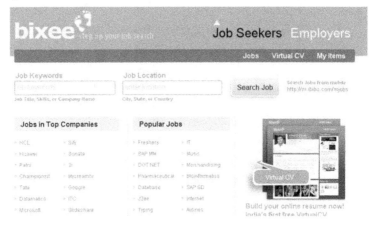

Jobs On Webdesignerwall

Design Jobs on the Wall — a job board managed by Web Designer Wall, where creative professionals come to find job opportunities. When you post your job here, it will be instantly featured on Web Designer Wall and others network sites where designers will see it. Due to website strong following, Web Designer Wall appears on loads of online portals and design publications.

Coroflot

Coroflot is an employment site for creative professionals – design firms post job openings and designers post portfolios – Coroflot makes the connection. Career and hiring advice, portfolio tips, how to find a design job and design salary surveys make Coroflot a valuable resource for the design community.

Freelanceswitch Jobs

Catering to the demands of all freelance professionals, this site is not just another place to find projects or seek the best of the manpower. Instead, it also serves as an information bank for freelancers and clients, providing them tips for easy and beneficial dealing as well as a healthy and interactive work environment.

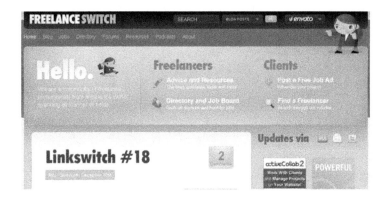

Designm.Ag

Array of designers and developers can now find full-time or freelance jobs all over the world in just a few clicks. Thank to Designm, talented professionals of the industry are now paid for what they are worth of and no longer have to toil to bag a handful of small and not-so-lucrative projects.

Lime Exchange

Making the ends meet between freelance talent and small or big scale businesses all over the world, Limeexchange allows professionals to not only find lucrative opportunities or get work done but also interact with one another at QnA platform and share recommendations and tips globally, about their respective industries.

Crowd Spring

What makes Crowdspring different is that it doesn't feel like a marketplace. You're not trying to outbid each other with a better price. You're not competing against others who have a better portfolio. How you approach a project, and how creative you really are is what can get you that project. You still get to compete with others, but it's a healthy kind of competition. You put up your design to win the project, and not your price.

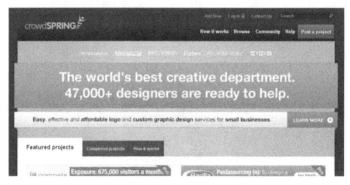

IFreelance

Your need may be of an experienced professional or an affordable novice, this is the place to find the top-notch photographers, web designers, proofreaders, data entry, bookkeeping and other such skilled freelancers. Freelancers are also free to choose projects that cater to their interest. What more? You need not bother to pay commissions to any mediator.

People Per Hour

Based on the simple bidding system, hire efficient freelancers here and enjoy the on-demand flexibility while saving money at the same time. Marketing, legal, accounting, writing, programming are some of the most common industry types covered by this site.

Krop

Krop is a Job Board and career resource website for creative professionals. Whether you're looking for job, or hunting top-notch talent, Krop's simple and powerful tools are geared towards connecting the worlds brightest minds with the best companies.

Sologig

Bridging the gap between experienced employees and qualified employers, this site is known to have the best talent in varied industries. You can seek both part-time and full-time contracts as well as consulting opportunities that nurture your talent further while filling your pockets.

Joomlancers

All Joomla professionals an now jump with joy as here is the site that caters to different work aspects of Joomla. Come and find work that adds more to your credibility as a Joomla professional and also reward you with a great sum.

Journalism Jobs

This is your best pick if your industry type is journalism and you wish to associate with a magazine, news group, radio, TV or any other type of media. Besides, you may also stay updated with the latest happenings of the industry with the news feeds and articles that are uploaded on the site.

Authentic Jobs

Creative and web professionals can seek reputed full-time and freelance opportunities here and get associated with well-known names of the industry like Sony BMG, HBO, HP, Facebook and many more.

GoFreelance

Now it's easy to market your freelance services and find all the
business you need to succeed. Gofreelance have thousands of
jobs in database, with fresh contracts and projects being added
daily. So kickstart your work-at-home career by signing up for
the free edition of The Freelance Job Report to get: Hot jobs and
cool projects emailed to you daily and a free 10-day course: 'The
Secrets of Freelance Success'.

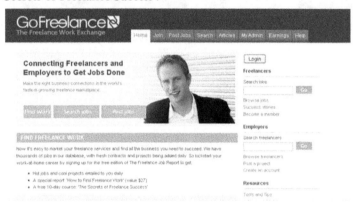

Freelance Designers

Industrial designer, advertising design, video <u>production</u>, architects, SEO, web designers and programmers are the primary categories at this job site for freelancers. Divided to precision into several sub categories, you can find your relevant category under the above listed major categories, to seek or provide suitable work.

LogoMyWay

Get an ideal logo designed for your company or website here. Let thousands of eminent professionals compete to get rewarded with your offered sum and in turn provide you gamut of logo choices to choose from. The minimum amount for which you can host a contest here is $200.

Freelancer.Co.Uk

Empowered by Escrow, this is another reliable site for freelancers. Get started from the marketplace or open or participate in contests, this exclusive site also contains several unusual categories like sourcing & manufacturing, multimedia & media, child care and system administration along with the famous freelance categories such as writing, translation, photography and others.

AllFreelanceWork

This is a true freelancers den with relevant portfolio creation and job site, all available at one place. In short, you learn as you earn.

Pro-Freelance

Pro-Freelance is a platform where freelancers can find all freelance projects from most important sites and the projects owners can find best experts at the best price. you can also freely propose your services on our classified page.

FreelanceWebmarket

Thousands of <u>freelance</u> programmers web designers web developers and many other proffesionals from the United States, United Kingdom, Canada, India and many other countries, expose your ad to 1000s of professionals. You can outsource worldwide or require professional from your country on FreelanceWebmarket and cut your expenses just paying a small fee.

WordPress Freelance

WordPress is indeed the best blog hosting site. Come and get your wordpress blog designed and programmed by eminent professionals of the field.

FreelanceWriting

As the name suggests, this site is a hub for those earning a living by writing. From reading tips on different writing styles, participation in writing contests to finding the high end freelance writing projects and career options available to writers, you can find it all here. This is what we call freelancing with a difference.

Php-Freelancers

Php-Freelancers is a "One stop " full service site where a Service buyer can post a project for free and have one of Php-Freelancers highly skilled freelancer's competitively bid on your projects. Php-Freelancers offers you the confidence that our freelancer's can meet your project needs no matter how small or large the project is.

Webdirections Jobs

Another online job portal dedicated to web professionals, here you can find jobs at full-time, freelance, part-time or even contractual basis.

Jsninja Jobs

A great site to apply for jobs in US, UK, Canada and other such developed countries. You may also find freelance work here in the fields for developers, designers and writers.

Bidhire

With no freelancer or buyer costs, bidhire gains an upper hand as compared to several other websites like Scriptlance, Elance and many others that charge a sign up fee from buyers and freelancers to post projects or start bidding respectively.

DesignCrowd

DesignCrowd is a graphic design marketplace that gives creative people opportunities. Businesses can post Open Brief Design Contests or Request Quotes for logo design, business card design, advertising artwork and website design.

Freelance-Projects

Freelance-Projects can be a great resource to help you mine for the experts you need to complete your next project. You can do this by simply using their search engine to find posted projects that are similar to what you are wanting to do or those that require the same technologies or programming language expertise that are required for your project.

Programmer Meet Designer

This is quite a unique online job portal, made exclusively for programmers and designers. Here, professionals from the two industries can collaborate with one another and share ideas to create websites that outperform all others, in design and functionality.

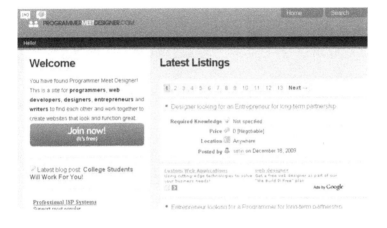

FreelancingJob

Webmasters need to have several jobs put together to frame a compelling website. This includes copy-writing, website designing, coding, web developer and several others. Find them all at this emerging online platform.

FreshWebJobs

FreshWebJobs is an online listing of web jobs. It is a site with a simple purpose and simple web site. It is well-designed, letting you know upfront how many jobs exist in different categories. It is still very young website, but very perspective. Currently are available 24 jobs.

AllDevJobs

This site caters to all kinds of professionals who belong to the development and designing jobs in some way or the other. Again, both freelance and full-time jobs are up for grab.

http://www.hongkiat.com/blog/50-freelance-job-sites-for-designers-programmers-best-of/

ONLINE DATA ENTRY JOBS: 9 LEGIT COMPANIES YOU CAN WORK FOR FROM HOME

Satrap Darabi, Yahoo Contributor Network

Jan 2, 2014

Legitimate data entry jobs are pretty much one of the first work-from-home types of jobs that most telecommuters have in mind, and for the right reasons. Data entry jobs can be done right from the comfort of your own home, and in all honesty, data entry jobs are not that hard to do. With most data entry jobs, just a minimum of computer skills is all that's needed to get the job done.

What is Data Entry?

Data entry is actually a broad term that describes a whole host of occupations, such as typists, word processors, transcribers, electronic data processors, coders and clerks. As you can see it includes lots of jobs that could be described as virtual assistant jobs .

Normally, data entry jobs are done through micro-labor companies that hire either interdependent contractors or employees to get the job done.

To explain data entry in a simpler term, you could say data entry means operating equipment (normally a keyboard), that inputs alphabetic, numeric, or symbolic data into a company's system. This data may need to be verified or edited as needed by the data entry worker.

Now, although all the data entry occupations I mentioned above are technically considered data entry work, advertised data entry jobs on the Internet normally require the least amount of skills, and obviously pay the least as well.

Data Entry Salary

Obviously, when it comes to salary and how much you can make as a data entry clerk, the company you get hired by, your location, the specific data entry position, experience and skills, can all have a big impact. But the average salary for data entry jobs according to SimplyHired.com is somewhere around $34,000. With the typical hourly rate for a Data Entry Clerk in the U.S. being anywhere between $9.84 to $13.43.

Data Entry jobs Scams

Unfortunately, work at home scam also expand to data entry jobs as well. So, you will have to be careful when looking for legit data entry jobs.

Differentiating between legit <u>data entry work</u> from home jobs and scams takes some research and a bit of common sense. Obviously, when you see a data entry job that promises you huge payouts that makes it look too good to be true, common sense should tell you stay away from it.

I mean, why would a job like data entry that pays an average around $12 an hour, would pay $50 an hour, like some data entry scams claim!?… I know you don't want to hear this, but legit data entry positions are often low paying jobs.

Data entry scams are usually the same as any other work at home scam type of scams. And they all have one thing in common, all of them will try to get money out of you one way or another. Whether it's through bogus classes, pyramid schemes, fake certifications or payment for resources that can be found for free on the web, they will try to make you pay.

That said, normally, data entry scams come in a few different forms:

- **Classes, Training, Kits, Certification**
  This is the most used form of work at home scam that unfortunately is used by data entry scammers as well. Some data entry scams will try to sell you classes and special courses that will "help you get certified", which will supposedly enable you get a job. In some cases,they tell you that the company you are going to work for actually requires you to take that class, and needless to say, you have to pay for the class. It is important to note that although many specialized data

entry jobs, such as medical or legal transcription do require special training, most basic data entry jobs do not.

- **Transcription Jobs**

   Although transcription is one form of data entry, scammers often will ask for a fee for "paid training" or a list of available employers. While many legit data entry jobs will require training and tests, with these scams, no one will ever pass the tests. But the scam company will "get a job for a nominal fee"!

- **Medical Coding and Transcription**

   Another form of data entry scam is done by scammers pretending they have medical coding jobs available for you. But you must pay to get a bogus certification or training.

- **High Paying Data Entry**

   As I mentioned above, legit data entry jobs are unfortunately, low paying jobs. So, if you see a company promising huge pay outs for it, it is a scam!

- **Process Rebates Scam**

   They advertise it as a job where you can make money easily by simply filling out online forms. This is the classic bait-and-switch scam. Once they convince you, you will be asked to pay $150-$200 for "access to work" which will enable you to "process rebates at home" and make money. But in reality, all you get is just information about finding jobs (that could be found for free with a little research), and not an actual job.

9 Legit Data Entry Companies

In order to make your job a little easier, I went on the hunt, and did some research to find a few trusted and legit companies that offer data entry online jobs .

As you may know, most data entry scam jobs charge you a fee to "give you work", and that's their scam. But most legit data entry companies are free to join. Doing data entry work for the companies mentioned below will not cost you a dime. You simply apply for the job, and if hired, you get paid for completing the job.

With that said, here is a list of 9 legitimate data entry job companies that you can work for:

1- Axion Data Services

You will be working as an independent contractor. Data entry jobs at Axion Data Services is done by independent contractors who are paid on a per-piece basis. They accept application whenever there are data entry jobs available.

2- Scribie

You can get hired as a freelancer to transcribe audio files with a length of about 6 minuets at a rate of about $10 per hour.

3- Clickworker

Clickworker is a famous international crowdsourcing company that hires independent contractors for data entry jobs. They also offer writing jobs, translation jobs, as well as research related tasks. ClickWorker pays on a per piece basis. Before you can begin working for CW, you must register and pass an assessment review to qualify.

4- DionData Solutions

If you have basic computer skills and can type with a minimum of 60 wpm, you are just what this company is looking for. There is no fee involved here.

5- DriverGuide

DriverGuide is basically a websites that offers computer drivers and support info. They hire database helpers from the U.S. and Canada, though you must have some specialized computer related skills. Your job would be updating databases of manufacturer and device drivers.

6- Working Solutions

They do both data entry and call centerjobs . You will be hired as an independent contractor. Although the company hires people from around the world for data entry jobs, usually U.S. applicants are more preferred for call center jobs are

7- VirtualBee (formerly Key For Cash)

They have an evaluation process that all applicants have to go through. If you are one of the lucky ones who passes the evaluation process with flying colors, you will be put on a waiting list to be contacted whenever work as available.

You can expect to get 40-55 cents per 1000 keystrokes. There is a minimum requirement for cashing out which is $50. The data you will be entering is all encoded data, so it appears nonsensical. This company is somewhat of an international data entry that hires from the U.S and most other countries.

8- QuickTate or iDictate

iDictate is a partner of QuickTate. They provide voice mail and other audio files transcription services, by employing work at home transcribers. You can earn 1 cent per 4 words with QuickTate, and 1 cent per 2 words with iDictate. If you prove your skills with QuickTate, you may get lots of jobs from iDictate which offers transcription work on a much wider range of documents. Successful QuickTate transcriptionist is may receive work from iDictate, which transcribes a wider range of documents.

9- TigerFish

Tigerfish is a company that has been in business since 1989. If you are a quick typist, you can make good money transcribing documents for Tigerfish. You can send an application via email.

Please do keep in mind that because of the nature of data entry, some of the companies mentioned above only have part time data entry jobs, and some don't always have positions available. Which means, they only hire when they have jobs available. So, it wouldn't hurt to bookmark this page, so you can check back with each company once in a while so you don't miss any legitimate online data entry jobs.

http://voices.yahoo.com/online-data-entry-jobs-9-legit-companies-work-12455308.html?cat=3

ARE YOU ON THE RIGHT CLOUD COMPUTING CAREER PATH?

David S. Linthicum, Contributor
Published: 28 Feb 2013

- E-Mail
- A
- AA
- AAA
- inShare41
- Facebook
- Twitter
- Share This
- RSS
- Reprints

ESSENTIAL GUIDE

NEED-TO-KNOW IT JOB REQUIREMENTS

- This article is part of an Essential Guide, our editor-selected collection of our best articles, videos and other content on this topic. Explore more in this guide:

2. - IT CAREERS AND THE CLOUD: READ MORE IN THIS SECTION

- **Get on the right cloud computing career path**
- IT departments to shrink dramatically within five years as cloud accelerates
- Third platform IT job skills in demand
- **Explore other sections in this guide:**
- 1. - Data center job requirements shift
- 3. - New IT certifications
- 4. - Job reduction and expansion news

While the rise of cloud computing frightens some in IT, many see the technology as an opportunity to accelerate their careers and bolster their bank accounts.

And IT pros have good reason to be optimistic. In a 2012 survey conducted within a 90-day period by Wanted Analytics, more than 2,400 companies said they are seeking candidates with cloud computing skills. Moreover, hiring demand increased by 61% from 2011 to 2012 for IT people with cloud knowledge. Analyst firm IDC also released a report last year that indicated public and private spending in cloud computing will increase exponentially over the next few years, resulting in an available jobs boost of nearly 14 million positions worldwide.

David S. Linthicum, cloud computing expert and consultant

There is an explosion in both the use of cloud computing and the demand for people to assist in the mass migration to cloud. Indeed, there are about 50 to 70 jobs chasing truly qualified candidates at this point in time, according to technical recruiters.

And there are two categories of cloud computing careers that seem to be emerging in the space: positions seeking IT pros with specific cloud skills and positions looking for IT admins with cloud architecture know-how.

Jobs that require specific cloud computing skills, such as Amazon Web Services (AWS) expertise or Google App Engine development skills, are typically with companies that have already committed to specific cloud service providers. These are usually for newly formed groups within IT departments, and the position is focused around tactical solutions development.

Roles for people with specific cloud skills encompass the majority of cloud computing jobs on the market today -- with AWS skills leading by a large margin, and Google, Microsoft and Rackspace postings following. Figure 1 shows the growth of job postings that request AWS talent, with a 2,500% growth over the six-year period. These jobs range from configuration, to development, to operations positions. And salaries range from $80,000 to $180,000 annually, depending on location.

Companies with positions for cloud architects seek people who can <u>define the cloud</u> -- from business requirements to the actual cloud deployment. These jobs tend to be with companies that have yet to define their path to the cloud and need some assistance in doing so. They may be defining the use of existing private and public clouds, or perhaps building clouds from the ground up.

Cloud architecture jobs are typically posted as "cloud solution architect" or other descriptive terms. Job posters are looking for strategic knowledge of most cloud computing technology and providers, and the ability to form those clouds to fit enterprise goals or needs.

Cloud architecture candidates should have enterprise architecture and/or service-oriented architecture experience, with some knowledge of the proper use of cloud computing technology. Salaries range from $100,000 to $200,000 annually, depending on location.

What you need to land that hot, new cloud job

With the rise of cloud-related jobs comes the rise of <u>cloud certification programs</u>. Larger cloud computing technology providers and vendors, such as IBM and Microsoft, as well as independent training organizations such as Cloud School and Learning Tree, typically offer these programs. Top cloud certification programs include:

- <u>IBM Certified Solution Advisor -- Cloud Computing Architecture</u>
- <u>IBM Certified Solution Architect -- Cloud Computing Infrastructure</u>
- <u>Microsoft Learning</u>
- <u>Google Apps Certified Deployment Specialist</u>
- <u>VMware Certified Professional (VCP)</u>
- <u>Certified Cloud Professional (CCP)</u>

As you may expect, technology providers tend focus on their own products. However, they do provide the basics around cloud computing architectures. If you are someone that learns through this type of training and needs that piece of paper, then these cloud certification programs might work for you.

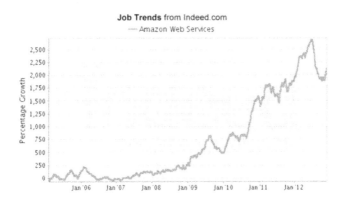

The majority of IT pros working in specific cloud positions either learned on the job or are self-taught. That may change as these types of programs become more popular, and employers require the certifications.

While cloud administrators can find what they need in the way of certifications, those looking for cloud architecture skills may be disappointed. General cloud computing courses typically focus on the very basics -- the difference between IaaS, SaaS and PaaS -- not on gory details, such as different approaches to building multi-tenant architecture, identity-based security and application programming interface design.

While most architects in the world of cloud computing also typically acquire their skills on the job, that could change as the certification programs become more comprehensive in the coming years.

Investing in cloud computing skills and knowledge seems to be a good bet today -- and a wise career move. While many IT admins will seek cloud skills and knowledge through training and certification programs, the reality is cloud computing is moving too fast for those programs to keep up.

David (Dave) S. Linthicum is the CTO and founder of Blue Mountain Labs, an internationally recognized industry expert and thought leader, and the author and co-author of 13 books on computing, including the best-selling Enterprise Application Integration. *Dave keynotes at many leading technology conferences on cloud computing, SOA, enterprise application integration and enterprise architecture.*

His latest book is <u>Cloud Computing and SOA Convergence in Your Enterprise, a Step-by-Step Guide</u>. *Dave's industry experience includes tenures as CTO and CEO of several successful software companies and upper-level management positions in Fortune 100 companies. In addition, he was an associate professor of computer science for eight years and continues to lecture at major technical colleges and universities, including the University of Virginia, Arizona State University and the University of Wisconsin.*

<u>http://searchcloudcomputing.techtarget.com/feature/Are-you-on-the-right-cloud-computing-career-path</u>

30 INCREDIBLE JOB SITES FOR FREELANCE COMPUTER TECHS

Published by ADMIN

With the spread of computer technology, it's a fairly good bet that those who have <u>computer science degrees</u> and information technology degrees will be in demand for a long time to come. Indeed, a computer technician who is knowledgeable about different systems can usually find a job.

And, these days, you don't even need to work for the same company for years and years. Instead, you can actually freelance, providing your services to a variety of companies. You might even be able to <u>make more money</u> as a freelance computer technician. Our connectedness as a society means that you should be able to find a number of opportunities online. If you are looking for a job as a freelance computer technician, here are 30 great places to start:

Computer and Technology Job Sites

Check out these job sites aimed specifically at helping those with skills in computers and in technology. Some of these are freelance jobs, as well as distance jobs that can be performed no matter where you are. Check out these sites for a good start.

1. Dice: This is *the* place to go if you are a technology professional. From computer jobs to IT jobs to everything in between, you can get access to great job opportunities as a freelancer.
2. Computer Jobs: Look here for jobs as a computer technician, or as some other type of computer professional. Includes freelance jobs and temporary jobs.
3. ComputerWork: If you are technically minded and good with computers, this is a great web site for you. Helpful for freelancers as well as those looking for more permanent jobs.
4. TechCareers: Look for a career in technology with help from this site. Post your resume as a freelance computer technician, and look for openings.
5. JustTechJobs: Connect with those who could use your skills. Great place for computer technicians to start, freelance or otherwise.

6. <u>Technology.Jobs</u>: Use this site to kickstart your job as a computer technician.

7. <u>Pathways to Technology</u>: A variety of different jobs dealing with computers, engineering and technology. A great resource for the freelance computer technician.

8. <u>Tech Centric</u>: Look for computer jobs on this web site aimed at technology and computers. Freelance jobs and temporary positions are available.

9. <u>Computer Tech Jobs</u>: No surprise here: These jobs are aimed at computer technicians. Plenty of work for the freelancer.

10. <u>KForce</u>: Find computer technician jobs all over the country, including jobs for freelancers.

Freelance Job Sites

Freelancing is on the rise, since technology has made it easier than ever to outsource work. Plus, with the recent recession, many employers are finding that freelancers can fill their needs. Freelance web sites offer to connect all types of freelancers with the companies that need their services. Visit these sites to look for freelance jobs in computers and technology.

11 <u>Guru.com</u>: This freelance marketplace allows you to bid on freelance projects in your area of expertise as a computer technician. A helpful place to start looking.

12. <u>Sologig</u>: Freelance web site that includes help finding freelance computer technician jobs, as well as IT and engineering jobs. A good place to start your search for a computer or technology related freelance gig.

13. <u>Flex Jobs</u>: You can find freelance work and part time work using this web site. A great place to look if you are searching for jobs that are a little more flexible.

14. <u>GoFreelance</u>: Another freelance marketplace that helps you find technology and computer jobs. A number of great freelance opportunities for the thoughtful freelancer.

15. <u>Elance</u>: Start here to find online freelance jobs for computer technicians and experts. Plenty of work to go around.

16. <u>iFreelance</u>: Find jobs with the help of this web site. You can freelance from anywhere, and highlight your skills as a computer tech.

17. <u>Project 4 Hire</u>: Use this web site to look for work as a computer technician. Plenty of tech and computer jobs available.

18. <u>Freelancer.com</u>: Just what it sounds like — you look for freelance work online. You find employers looking for contract workers in a number of fields, including computer tech.

19. <u>All Freelance Directory</u>: Not only can you find freelance jobs here, but you can also get access to helpful articles and tips about freelancing. A solid resource for freelance computer technicians.

20. <u>Odesk</u>: There are a number of freelance jobs available through this web site. You can find a position as a contract computer technician, looking for temporary and freelance positions.

21. <u>Smashing Jobs</u>: Look for great jobs all over the world. Includes computer jobs, technician jobs and other technology opportunities. A great place to find the right job for you.

22. <u>Sitepoint Market</u>: Another freelance market place where you can sell your skills as a computer technician. Let others know your qualifications, and look for the right job for you. This is a well known technology site.

23. <u>FreelanceSwitch</u>: Get paid as a contractor. Look for jobs, and find helpful information on pricing your services to clients. A great resource for the talented freelance computer technician.

General Job Sites

Increasingly, you can find temporary and freelance jobs on the larger job web sites. Don't think that you can't find what you're looking for on a more conventional and "traditional" job web site. Here are some sites that might be able to help you out.

24. <u>Technology Jobs and Resources</u>: Plenty of computer related and technology jobs on the Monster.com web site.

25. IT Jobs on CareerBuilder: A number of computer jobs, including computer technician jobs for freelancers and temporary workers. A great place to start your job search.

26. Technology Jobs: The Ladders offers access to high paying job leads. Visit the technology section to learn more about how you can connect with companies that need your computer technician skills.

27. Technology Jobs: Check with Indeed.com to find computer related jobs. Entry level, temporary and freelance opportunities.

28. Computer Jobs: Nation Jobs offers access to a variety of opportunities for the computer technician and other technology related jobs.

29. Technology Jobs: Simply Hired is another big-name job site that has jobs aimed at computer technicians and engineers.

30. Information Technology Jobs: Look for the right job for you at Thingamajob.com. Freelance positions are readily available as well.

<u>I HAVE BUILT A BUSINESS FROM</u>
<u>ONLINE FREELANCING</u>

"I wanted to do something great since my childhood. I wanted to be a computer geek. I did Computer Systems Engineering. While I started engineering, I started to find ways to make money online. I Googled the ways and tried many of them, from seeing advertisement for some seconds to blogging but there was not much money in it. It wasted 2 years of my life in searching for a way to earn money online. Blogging was the worst thing I ever did, 200 articles and no money made. I tried everything. Did the keyword researches, made plans, got investments and burnt those investments but did not made a penny.

Then I came across the concept of freelancing. A safer way to earn online. I started with a new $5 gig website and made some hundred dollars from it. It was fun, as I did not need to promote my gigs myself but I still got customers.

I made accounts on all the big freelance websites and started to bid. I had a portfolio. Luckily, I got some good clients at the start some which guided me towards improvement and told me how could I improve my work. I created a company website and made my brand. I kept on bidding on the websites.

The good thing with freelancing was that I could easily make a lot of money as the dollar conversion rate in Pakistan is good. This made me more focused on the project types and I could even choose among the projects which I wanted to do and which not.

I learnt SEO and did SEO work online. It was an excellent earning. Apart from SEO, I also used to do content writing. I wrote a lot of content for blogs and kept updating my old blog too, which improved my English.I also learnt all of the basic programming that can be done on the web and started to create small tools online. I chose PHP as the language of my choice. It was a good decision. It paid me off in various ways. I could now create things online myself.

Some of the bad times in freelancing career are when you get scammed. I got scammed a loT.Sometimes by the freelancing websites and sometimes by the clients. The problem with the clients are that many of them are over ambitious and have a vague idea of what they want to create. Another issue with freelancing is lack of confidence over the skills of the person who you are hiring. The ratings are easily bought. The clients are non-technical. They do not understand this. Until they get crap products after paying a lot of money. The reason, they had no experience of it.

One more issue with freelancing is in getting payments. When I started working, this was the biggest issue. This question came to my mind each and every time I did something online. I asked myself, "How am I going to get paid for it?", because there was no medium to get paid easily in Pakistan. I did research and found out that a Payoneer Card could be created which could be used to get payments in Pakistani banks. I applied for that card and when I got it, I transferred some money into that bank account. Guess what, I got my payment in hand!

One of the best times was when my company worked with Mobilezapp, a growing IT company in United States. I started out as their developer and then became their lead developer. As their lead developer, I served their new website and after that the reputation of my company become very good. Now, I am getting a lot of projects from oDesk. My fourth company, LigerLab now works for the world's leading IT companies. Thank you oDesk for making my life."

Fahad Uddin - Pakistan

6

FREELANCE MARKETING &PR

A guide to freelancing — media and PR

Fancy going freelance? According to our experts, being able to find good case studies and interviewees is an essential skill, a strong online presence is a must and you need dramatic ideas in order to catch an editor's eye. Here are the best bits from our live Q&A

- **Alison White**
- theguardian.com, Monday 26 July 2010 16.02 BST

Tracy Playle is a communications consultant who specialises in advising the education sector on the use of social and digital media for PR and marketing activities through her company, Pickle Jar Communications

Your employer might support your move to freelance and become one of your clients: My former employer before I went it alone was actually my very first client and I continue almost three years on to work for them on and off. They're likely to be one of the first people to recommend you to others if they value your work too. It's worth remembering that there's nothing wrong with wanting to try a different approach to working. Try to put a positive stance on it — for me freelancing and consultancy made more sense because I'm much more of a project person and get itchy feet if I do the same thing for too long, so if you can identify the positive reasons why you think this is a better fit for you rather than why you aren't happy in your current role, then they will undoubtedly be supportive.

Accountants are worth their weight in gold: The first advice I give to anyone is to get yourself a good accountant from day one (or even before then — mine asked me some very challenging questions that really helped me to assess that I was doing the right thing). They're worth their weight in gold in terms of advising on company structure (I opted for VAT-registered limited company, for example, instead of sole trader) and they take away all the hassle of knowing what's what in the very important tax world. I'm under strict instruction from my accountant to never ever upset HM Revenues and Customs.

Don't forget the added value a full-time role can give you at the start of your career: Working for an employer might provide you with training opportunities that you wouldn't be able to afford if working for yourself (attending conferences, workshops, further study and so on) and allow you to develop a niche and a good network of contacts. Don't rule out freelancing but don't forget the added value that a full-time role will give you when you set out.

Olivia Gordon is a freelance journalist who writes for national newspapers, women's magazines, websites and specialist publications. Together with fellow freelancer Johanna Payton, she teaches freelance *journalism courses for <u>Olivia and Johanna Training</u> and <u>Journalism. co.uk</u>*

What you charge can depend on the size of the publication: In terms of fees, the <u>National Union of Journalists' website</u> has a useful freelance fees guide which tells you how much to charge as a minimum depending on the size of publication. If you are just starting out, you may have to do some low paid or unpaid writing to build up some cuttings, but once you have some good cuttings, you can generally expect to earn at least £300 for 1,000 words — if not considerably more.

Finding case studies and interviewees is a real skill: Finding case studies and interviewees is a real skill. Generally though it's a matter of common sense and being persistent. You can find someone to talk to you on virtually anything if you look hard enough. Googling, obviously, is a good idea, as are support groups, internet forums, press offices, charities, publishers, news agencies, and of course your friends and family — the list of places to look is endless.

Think of dramatic and exciting ideas to catch an editor's eye: It's just a matter of sending a good strong pitch on a fresh, original and topical idea. I find the mistake most newbies make is not coming up with ideas that are dramatic and exciting enough to make an editor think "Wow! I must commission this right away before anyone else does!" For example, ideas about redundancy and career changes (especially 'mumpreneurs') are two-a-penny these days, so to pitch something on this sort of topic with any hope of success, you'd need to come up with a killer angle which hasn't been covered before, or a red hot story.

Natalie Persoglio is a freelancer with more than 12 years experience in the marketing, journalism, PR and communications industries

HM Revenues and Customs run free short courses on tax issues: As I'm not naturally a numbers person I thought I would struggle with the financial aspect of freelancing, but there's a lot of information out there. I pretty much had my hand held through my first tax return, courtesy of HM Revenues and Customs. They run free, short courses (an afternoon) in most areas, so it's actually fairly straightforward.

Start building your freelance career while making the most of the security of a full-time position: I became exclusively freelance about three years ago, but before this I worked in full-time roles and ran freelance projects during out-of-office hours, evenings and weekends. It's actually the ideal position to be in, as you're building a career in freelance while still having the security of a full-time position.

Training is really important, but it can be hard to plan: On making time for developing skills through training as a freelancer — with freelance work often being quite spontaneous it can be difficult to make concrete plans such as committing to training, as you can miss out on jobs which pop up at the last moment or existing projects which need extra care. Training is really important, so I should really include it in my planning.

Derek Kelly is managing director of ClearSky Accounting, a firm specialising in accounting for freelancers, contractors and interim workers

Getting help with your finances can save you time and money: If you are in it for the long-term, then setting up a limited company will most likely provide you with the best net return as you can undertake some simple tax planning to minimise the amount of tax you pay. If you use a specialist firm of freelance accountants, then you will be surprised as to how little you have to do in terms of paperwork. I would guess about 30 minutes per week at most.

Catherine Quinn is a freelance writer with more than a decade of experience selling features to national publications. She is the author ofNo Contacts? No Problem! How to Pitch and Sell a Freelance Feature

Make the most of modern technology and get away from your desk: I do travel journalism and I am on the road a lot, and I have to say it really is very easy nowadays. Technology is a complete gift, and I could have kissed whoever invented internet telephones when I made my first call. I spent a month in China travelling round earning more or less the same as I would at my desk, conducting interviews at 10pm rather than 10am and writing it up via WiFi in hostels. God bless the internet, I say.

Katie Moffat is a freelance PR consultant specialising in online public relations and social media. She is also a trainer in online PR and social media for digital specialists Econsultancy

Putting effort into being visible online can pay off: It's vital that you are easily visible online. Definitely get a website that acts as a showcase and if you have the time, do start blogging — I would echo other comments on here that it's a great way to demonstrate your knowledge. For example, you could blog about dealing with the media, how to write a great news story and so on — lots of small businesses would be interested in that kind of subject. Set up a profile on <u>LinkedIn</u> and spend some time joining and contributing to groups. Definitely look at <u>Twitter</u> — I have had so much work as a result of being active on Twitter. And if you can, look at some of the business forums and contribute to threads. Although the results of online activity might not be immediate, it will pay off.

<u>Helen James</u> is the founder of <u>Freelance UK</u>, a community for creative and media freelancers

Make sure the freelance lifestyle suits you: I would recommend you work out what's important in terms of your lifestyle too. Freelancing may not be a steady stream of work, especially as you get your business off the ground. One of the benefits for employers is that they can often ask a freelancer for last minute work, over the weekend perhaps. So bear this in mind. Plenty of freelancers take on evening and weekend work initially before leaving their permanent job.

<u>http://careers.theguardian.com/a-guide-to-freelancing-media-and-pr</u>

THE VIRTUAL AGENCY MODEL LEADS TO CONCRETE BENEFITS

11 December 2013 by Richard Houghton,

Virtual comms agencies create real-world benefits for clients, staff and business owners alike.

Virtual teams mean virtual profits, right? You can't have your entire team working from home because they will take the dog for a walk or play *Grand Theft Auto V* all day. Anyway, you need an office so that clients can come in for meetings, coffee and biscuits.

Wrong. Early adopters across marketing services are thriving with the home-working virtual agency model. Robust and sustainable profits are being delivered by senior practitioners and clients are loving the results.

The virtual agency model may also be the answer to one of the biggest issues the PR agency sector faces: the loss of highly experienced and talented females in their late twenties and early thirties. We have been slow to find ways of bringing these valuable fee earners back into the workplace and have lost out as a result.

Tamara Littleton, founder and chief executive of eModeration, a multilingual social media management agency, has built her £8m business over the past 11 years on the virtual team model. With 350 people working in 50 languages for clients as diverse as HSBC and MTV, it has been a hugely successful model.

Working closely with agencies and directly with clients, Littleton's business demands senior community moderators who are able to understand the nuances of both their clients' brands and local cultural references. These experienced practitioners are attracted by the opportunity to use their skills on big brand campaigns while working from their home office.

Social animals

Human nature being what it is, most of us do not wish to work exclusively at home. So small eModeration hub offices allow team members to meet for ad hoc briefings, creative sessions and to get a social fix when needed. Another nice touch is a coffee and drinks allowance for staff travelling internationally to encourage them to get to know locally based colleagues.

One of the main criticisms of the virtual agency model is it does not allow for the provision of senior consultancy. But this doesn't fit with the experience of Littleton or Paul Moran, founder of marketing comms agency Switch. His employees each have, on average, more than ten years' experience and are seeking flexible, but not necessarily part-time, hours. Many work flexibly, allowing them to handle parenting commitments and balance other interests.

It is not just start-ups that are developing the networked agency model. Grayling UK has started to implement a hybrid model – a mix of office and home-working – at its Bristol office. Designed to meet demands for a more flexible working week, it was implemented following an analysis of time spent in the office by account teams. The result is a new office with lockers for all team members and clear desks to be used by any of the team as required. The benefit is motivated staff and margin improvement.

Client benefits

From the client perspective, the model appears to have been accepted, with Littleton and Moran initially shy of pushing how they operated. They now find it is seen as a benefit by clients as it allows for the rapid up and down scaling of resources, as work demands. This is particularly attractive as the amount of project work increases.

Technology should not be a barrier to running a networked agency. EModeration relies on off-the-shelf software services to provide the necessary secure log-in, databases, internal and client comms and video conferencing. Interestingly, eModeration's management can track not only when teams log in, but also where they log in, ensuring that confidential work is done at the home office and not the coffee shop. IT support is run on the same model, allowing for round-the-clock support.

There is no doubt it requires a different management approach to run a virtual agency than one that is based in physical offices. The learnings seem to be consistent. To paraphrase Lance Armstrong, it's not about the technology. Building a strong motivating culture with trust at its heart is the starting point. Due to the disparate locations of the team, management needs to almost over-communicate to make sure that the message gets through.

While it is highly unlikely we will move en masse to a networked model, there will be a shift to a hybrid model as Generation Y moves up the ranks and pressure on margins grows. More start-ups will adopt it to provide that much-vaunted life/work balance, while meeting client demands for senior advice and support on tap. Maybe we will stop losing experienced female consultants who quite rightly want to be able to balance work and family life.

Richard Houghton is associate partner at Agency People.

http://www.prweek.com/article/1220593/virtual-agency-model-leads-concrete-benefits

7

Freelance Admin/ Clerical Work

Work-From-Home Clerical Jobs Examined

Many **clerical jobs** are perfectly suited to working from home. With advances in technology making it so the masses own personal computers and have access to high-speed Internet connections, you probably have almost everything you need to perform clerical work from your home office.

What are Clerical Jobs?

Virtual assistants, bookkeepers, accounting jobs, typists and data entry jobs all fall under the general category of clerical jobs. These jobs usually involve performing the duties of a clerk or secretary, typing and entering data into software applications on a personal computer. Because of the lower cost of overhead and expenses involving employees, many businesses, large and small, are contracting out clerical jobs to people who work from home.

Required Skills

The skills required for clerical work will vary from job to job. At a minimum, you need to possess a basic aptitude for typing and working with computer software applications in order to be successful at clerical work. Some clerical jobs like bookkeeping may require further training or experience dealing with business finance. Accounting jobs often require a college degree as well as certification. To work as a virtual assistant, you may need a combination of skills involving typing, phone skills, basic bookkeeping skills and computer skills.

Required Equipment

The equipment required for most clerical jobs is a personal computer, high-speed Internet access and the standard office software applications that come with most home computer systems. Beyond that, your employer may use a specific software application that you don't already have. If you work as a virtual assistant, you may need a separate phone line or a headset. Your employer may also require that your home office setup has a door separating you from family disturbances during work hours.

Avoiding Scams

If you have looked online for work-from-home jobs, you probably already know that much of what you find is some sort of a scam. Or, at least, the job is not what it appears to be. If you look for clerical jobs online, be certain that they are just that: clerical jobs where you are hired by an employer.

You can get involved in paying for leads and information, but most legitimate jobs can be found for free by looking at local classified ads or websites like Elance, ifreelance and Career Builder that cater to freelancers and the work-from-home community. One sure way to be taken in by a scam is to buy into the hype that you can get rich performing simple clerical jobs. The truth is that if the job sounds too good to be true, then it probably is.

Expect that a legitimate company offering legitimate clerical work will pay you commensurate to the going rate for that type of work. If they are offering more, then beware and be sure to read the fine print before you give out any personal information.

Clerical jobs suited to telecommuting and remote home offices are available in abundance. With the right combination of clerical skills, home office setup and wariness toward work-from-home scams, you can find clerical work that is just right for you.

How to Become a Freelance PA or Administrator

http://www.easyaccountancy.co.uk/industry/businessmarketing/freelancer_self_employed_pa_administrator.html

The idea of working with a freelancer for admin support or PA services is a relatively new one. Traditionally this was a service which companies simply had to have in house, but with the advent of remote working technologies, email, video calling, online collaboration for diary management and so on – it's now entirely possible to have a 'virtual' or freelance admin support resource.

This type of service is especially useful for companies which are not really large enough to warrant a full time admin staff member or for senior managers who do not need a full time PA. In the same way as a **marketing freelancer** might work with multiple clients simultaneously, so a freelance administrator or freelance personal assistant can do exactly the same thing. It's quite normal in a business environment to have admin staff who are located in separate offices or even separate buildings from the people that they support, so what does it matter if the freelance equivalent is actually hundreds of miles away? The support service can be just as good.

Many PA's and Administrators start off doing a little **freelance work in their spare time** whilst still holding onto a full time job. If you're doing this or thinking of doing this it's probably a good idea to have a chat with an accountant as there may be tax implications you should be considering and maybe also allowances you aren't taking advantage of.

There are numerous **benefits to freelancing**, for example the freedom and flexibility to work for as many different types of client as you like as well as the obvious benefit of increasing your take home pay. In fact our **freelancer take home pay calculator** shows you how much you can expect to take home as a freelancer.

http://www.wahm.com/articles/work-from-home-clerical-jobs-examined.html

HOW TO BECOME A VIRTUAL ADMINISTRATIVE ASSISTANT

Virtual assistants require no standard educational background, but need a diverse range of skills.

A **virtual administrative assistant** is becoming a popular work-from-home job. This job takes the title of office assistant to a new level, by allowing the employee to perform the duties of administrative assistant from the comfort of their own home.

Typically, a virtual secretary performs tasks like:

- setting appointments
- transcription
- emailing and posting mail correspondences
- electronic filing
- word processing

If a career as a <u>virtual administrative assistant</u> sounds like the perfect opportunity for you, or if you are a current office assistant who wants to transition to working for home, try these tips on how to become a virtual administrative assistant.

Necessary Education

There is no blanket standard of educational requirements to be a virtual assistant. Educational requirements typically vary by employer depending on the employer's needs, the type of business that you work for and the specific project. Therefore, some employers may only require a high school diploma or equivalent degree, while others may want to hire a virtual secretary who has a four-year degree, or even a graduate degree.

Necessary Training

Many websites offer <u>virtual administrative assistant training</u> for a fee, but be wary of these websites. There is no nationally accredited virtual assistant training certification, and most employers will not ask whether you have some form of virtual assistant certification.

The majority of employers are more concerned with your level of experience, and what you can do to benefit their company. It is important to have a well-written resume, as well as excellent referrals and testimonials to validate the quality of your work.

The Proper Equipment

As with any career, you must have the proper equipment and resources to perform necessary tasks. Some of the necessary equipment needed to be a virtual administrative assistant is:

- Computer with a high speed Internet connection
- Printer/scanner/copier combo
- Fax machine
- One land line, although some jobs may require you to have two land line phone numbers
- A home office that promotes a proper work environment with little to no distractions

Hone Your Skills

Whether you are currently employed as an in office administrative assistant, or whether you are beginning an entirely new career as a virtual administrative assistant, it is important to polish your skills. Honing the skills necessary to be a virtual assistant will make your more attractive to potential employers. The following are some of the necessary skills needed to be a virtual secretary:

- Above average communication skills
- Ability to multitask, while thinking clearly and logically
- Excellent typing skills of 70 words per minute (wpm) or higher
- Have more than proficient skills in grammar and writing
- General computer knowledge including word processing, spreadsheets, databases and email

Post Your Resume on the Internet

Since you are going to become a virtual administrative assistant, one of the best ways to <u>find jobs</u> is to search the Web. You can browse tons of different job databases, and you can even post your resume online, as well. Some websites may charge a monthly service fee to use their resources, while others, like our <u>WAHM job board</u>, provide job listings for free.

Some online boards request that job seekers bid on specific virtual assistant jobs by listing their hourly work rate, or their fee for the completion of a specific project. Other databases allow virtual assistants to post their resumes online, so that employers may contact them about employment.

The best resources for job openings and resum posting for freelance virtual assistants include:

- indeed.com
- virtualassistants.com
- virtualassistantjobs.com
- virtual-assistant-advice.com

Explore Options with Your Current Employer

If you are currently employed outside of the home as an administrative assistant, but you would like to make the transition to working from home, ask your employer about your company's work from home options. In many cases, employers are willing to allow their administrative assistants to work from home, because it frees office and saves money in office expenses.

Shop Your Skills to Area Businesses

In addition to looking to the Internet or your current employer for virtual assistant jobs, you should talk to business owners in your area about the benefits of hiring you as a virtual assistant. By providing a letter of interest or cover letter, and your resume, you could essentially create a new job for yourself working from home as a virtual secretary for a local business.

If you have a good strategy and game plan for approaching local business owners, you could soon be a full-time employee or an independent contractor.

Networking and Professional Connections

When you become a virtual assistant, one of the best ways to continue to learn about your trade and expand your business contacts is to networkand make professional connections.

Some of the best ways to network and make professional connections include ideas like:

- Joining LinkedIn - an online resource where millions of working professionals exchange information and form business relationships
- Participating in online forums and message boards
- Joining professional networks like the International Virtual Assistants Association (IVAA)
- Regularlyvisitingorjoiningvirtualassistantnetworking. com and the Virtual Assistant Association

Networking not only allows you to build friendships, references and business contacts with other virtual assistants, but also allows you to make contact with potential employers.

http://www.wahm.com/articles/how-to-become-a-virtual-administrative-assistant.html

ONLINE COLLABORATION SOFTWARE: ARE VAS WORKING WELL IN THE CLOUD OR ARE THEIR HEADS JUST IN THE CLOUDS?

Online collaboration software seems to be catching on amongst the virtual assistants I know, but especially those who have multiple projects on the go or work in a multi-VA/multi-contractor environment. Yet, despite the productivity benefits of using programs like<u>Basecamp</u> or <u>ClientSpot</u>, a lot of VAs are saying it remains a challenge to get their clients on board.

I understand all to well. It's hard enough to remember to log in to the software I use *for my own company* let alone doing so as a client. I have one fab VA who works for me and uses Basecamp religiously. Yet I still can't seem to stop myself from sending quickie emails when I need something on the fly. Then again, maybe we're expecting too much from these programs. I mean, who over the age of 25 doesn't live and breathe email?

Maybe it's time to re-evaluate why we need or *think* we need to use online collaboration software in the first place. Then we can make a more informed decision as to whether it's worth both the expense and the effort to create long term buy in. To do this, we must look at both sides of the equation: VA and Client.

From the virtual assistant's perspective:

- Potentially how many hours a month of admin time will I save? Does this justify the monthly or yearly expense incurred?
- How much work will it be to get everyone on my team using the software consistently? Is it worth the effort?
- Do I want this to be an internal collaboration tool, much like a company intranet, or do I want to use the software as a way to more effectively engage my clients? Or both?
- Do my clients even care if we have these kinds of tools? Does it impress them or make them view me/my company as less freelance and more entrepreneur?
- Does the software offer functionality such as milestone tracking or contact management that could replace my existing tools offline?
- If the system goes offline for a period of time will business continuity be impacted?

And from the client's perspective:

- Am I paying competitive rates despite the software's cost of use?
- If I'm paying a premium for my virtual assistant services, what are the value adds? Increased productivity? More effective communication? Peace of mind? Faster data retrieval?
- What are the potential drawbacks of adjusting to "working in the cloud?"

- Can you make a convincing case for me to change from email thinking to "log in" thinking (i.e. working in the cloud versus working in the hard drive)?
- What if I just don't want to work collaboratively online, period? What's your policy on this? For example, can you work internally on my project in the cloud but work with me via email and phone?

These are just some of the questions swimming in my head of late as I try to make my own collaborative processes more efficient. Right now, I am using <u>Backpackit</u> as a company intranet, no clients allowed. And for the moment, it is working, though not as well I hope it will function for my team in the future. I'm tempted to bring my clients onside, but then I have to think about the whole privacy and "play nice while the client is watching" thing. When I was using Basecamp I found this a bit onerous. Not because we're a bunch of potty mouthed VAs and consultants, but because having to constantly remember who is privy to the conversation thread and who is cumbersome and even squelches free thinking at times.

Therein lies the rub. As a client, do you want to be part of a collaborative environment all or most of the time? Not always having say as to who is privy to the conversation thread you've just been pulled into? Do you feel more or less in control when a discussion is primarily taking place via email? Or do you find a VA who uses online collaboration software to actually be more professional, more organized, more on top of things?

- See more at: http://www.vanetworking.com/clients/online-collaboration-software-are-vas-working-well-in-the-cloud-or-are-their-heads-just-in-the-clouds/#sthash.hgoMZt6p.dpuf

http://www.vanetworking.com/clients/online-collaboration-software-are-vas-working-well-in-the-cloud-or-are-their-heads-just-in-the-clouds/

KEEP TRYING AND YOU WILL GET THERE!

"Working online is one of the most challenging yet rewarding experiences. One gets to plan for their time and negotiate for their payment terms. I was a full time employee and after giving birth to my twin boys, my husband and I decided that I should be a stay at home mum so that our children would get the best parental care. Being a full time mum posed a challenge because I was employed and I could contribute towards the running of the home. We now depended on my husband income but nevertheless he still remained very supportive.

A mutual friend of the family introduced me to online working on oDesk. She told me that I could still be a stay at home wife and still make a decent living doing online work. I always had a passion for writing and doing online research. I bought a laptop and started looking for opportunities online as a freelance writer and editor.

The internet was full of opportunities but the biggest challenge was differentiating between the genuine tasks from the scams. It was not easy starting out because most of the clients would promise instant riches. Others would request you to pay for a membership in their sites so that they could give you lots of work. Once you subscribed they could just give you a handful of jobs and keeping their promise of providing constant work turned to be very elusive. In my naivety I believed in all these lies and did as I was told.

I landed my first job on oDesk after several weeks of searching, which was online Captcha data entry. These types of jobs are the worst online because they promise to pay you thousands of dollars and make you a millionaire overnight. The client gives you a test job to complete only for you to realize that you have been scammed. They give several people different parts of the task as a test job and before you know it you have worked for free. Some clients would just refuse to pay you after working for them. They would disappear after they got their tasks completed. I was discouraged that I almost gave up on my online career. I turned to freelance online forums and oDesk support to discuss about my nasty experiences. Through other people's experience, and support staff on oDesk, I was able to relate to my own challenges and this made me to start appreciating that I could make a living just like any person who was employed full time.

I landed my first job on oDesk and realized that there are still honest people in the world. The client was from a different culture from mine. I had to learn how to address people by their names and communicate effectively without sounding offensive. The best lesson that I learnt is that communication with the client was key if I wanted to succeed in my online career. I also learnt keeping promises and finishing the work within the stipulated deadlines ensured that the clients trusted me more. I started getting repeat clients and referrals from people I had worked for before and were happy with my work. After my first contract, I was rated 5* by the client and this increased my marketability in the online world. I learnt that there are amazing people out there who are willing to break cultural and language barriers and work with anyone across the world. Online working has made me a better person and a very good communicator both in the real and online world. I have become more understanding and very patient because not everyone will move with my pace of doing things. People are different and they should be treated with empathy and respect."

- Grace Muchiri -

8

FREELANCE SALES/ SUPPORT/TELESALES

What Is Inside Sales? The Definition Of Inside Sales

Ken Krogue**Contributor**

The most pragmatic definition of Inside Sales is simple: **inside sales is remote sales.**

It has been called virtual sales, professional sales done remotely, or one of my recent favorites "sales in the cloud." Where outside sales or traditional field sales is done face-to-face.

Taken in this context, the majority of *all* sales is done remotely, and the numbers are growing. The most recent <u>Lead Management study</u> found that over the past three years, inside sales grew at a fifteen times higher rate (7.5% versus .5% annually) over outside sales, to the tune of 800,000 new jobs. (Note, another market size study is underway and should be available shortly.)

More evidence: if you don't believe it, grab a list of 10 traditional or "outside sales" people and call them. 6 out of 10 will be sitting in front of their computer, working in their cubicle, office, or home office—just like the inside sales people. They may not answer as fast as inside sales reps would, but leave a message and they will call you back. Outside sales is converging into inside sales, or as my friend Bob Perkins, the CEO and Founder of The American Association of Inside Sales Professionals said, "Inside sales is just... sales."

The term "inside sales" originally came about in the late 1980s as an attempt to differentiate "telemarketing" (or "telesales" in the UK) from the more complex, "high-touch," phone-based business-to-business (B2B) and business-to-consumer (B2C) selling practices.

Telemarketing is often believed to have begun in the 1950s by DialAmerica Marketing, Inc., reported to be the first company dedicated to telephone sales and services. By the 1970s telemarketing was a common phrase used to describe the process of selling over the telephone. It often included both outbound and inbound, but later became much more synonymous with the types of outbound calling we're all familiar with—large-scale "blasts" to lists of names to try and drum up quick sales, usually while the family is sitting around the dinner table.

By the late 1990s/early 2000s, inside sales was the term used to differentiate the practice from outside sales—the traditional face-to-face sales model where salespeople went to the client's location of business to engage in the sales process.

In 2004, when Dave Elkington and I founded InsideSales. com, we searched the keyword "inside sales" on Google **GOOG** +2.64% and there was nobody else there. However, there were tens of thousands of companies that came up trying to hire inside sales reps. What was a second class department is now the fastest growing segment of sales and lead generation. With the American Association of Inside Sales Professionals (AA-ISP), a viable inside sales industry association in place for five years, inside sales is an industry rapidly maturing.

Companies found the new channel of inside sales to be undeniably effective, but often didn't know what to do to solve the conflict between the younger, disruptive, more technically savvy upstarts who sold over the phone, and their more senior counterparts who wielded incredible political power in their organizations as the entrenched source of revenue for nearly a century.

For years, inside sales has been relegated to generating leads for the more senior outside sales reps or merely closing the smaller accounts. This is now no longer the case. Many companies are already using a hybrid form of inside sales, with reps calling from their company's home office, then traveling occasionally to client locations and merely calling it "sales." Research shows that four years ago, outside sales reps spent 41 percent of their day selling remotely. Two years ago it rose to 46 percent. It is now crossing 50 percent.

By <u>Marc Benioff</u>'s own admission in his book <u>*Behind the Cloud*</u>, salesforce.com "grew their company for the first five or six years with a telesales [or inside sales] model." They added outside sales or field sales to go upmarket when they wanted to sell to <u>Enterprise</u>-class companies, but the company still does a majority of their innovative sales work remotely. We know because we hired Dave Orrico, the Executive Vice President who started the enterprise division of salesforce.com, to join us at InsideSales.com.

True door-to-door field sales is almost extinct, and has of necessity become a hybrid by our definition.

What technology can be credited for creating inside sales?

The phone?

No.

It was Webex and GoToMeeting by Citrix.

It was web conferencing, or the ability to demonstrate products remotely that put inside sales on the map.

The phone created telemarketing which was a precursor to inside sales. But the greatest increases in productivity have come with internet technology, hosted CRM, social media, immediate response, local presence, and telephony tools integrated together.

We call these "power tools" for sales people.

Would you try to build a house with a hammer when you have a nail gun?

Marc Benioff started salesforce.com using Inside Sales during the First 6 Years - (AP Photo/Ben Margot, File)

Another way of defining inside sales is to also state what it is not.

Inside sales is not telemarketing.

Let me repeat: *inside sales is NOT telemarketing.*

Telemarketing is a scripted, single-call-close, almost always targeting a small-ticket, business to consumer (B2C) model.

Inside sales is not scripted. It requires multiple calls or "touches" to create a sales close, involves medium or large ticket goods and services, and targets business-to-business (B2B) or high-end business-to-consumer (B2C) transactions.

Inside sales is *professional* sales done remotely or virtually. It is not the mindless "phone drone" that calls at dinner time and won't hang up until you have said "no" seven times. Telemarketing uses dated predictive dialing technology which helped drive such a negative mindset in consumers that laws were passed regulating their use. Inside sales uses power dialing technology that moves the more sophisticated "predictive 2.0" technology into the data using predictive analytics, big data, and machine learning to improve on the older technology by removing the stigma of abandoned calls of the overused technology.

To true <u>inside sales professionals</u>, the "tele" of telemarketing is a four letter word.

Inside sales is also not customer service. Though inside sales frequently involves an element of inbound call handling like a customer service department, in its pure form it is not customer service.

Some companies erroneously describe their inbound call centers as "inside sales," but this does not fall within the boundaries of our definition unless the agents' primary function is selling.

Inside sales is professional sales done remotely. . . it is remote sales.

Author: <u>Ken Krogue</u>

http://www.forbes.com/sites/kenkrogue/2013/02/26/what-is-inside-sales-the-definition-of-inside-sales/

SALES JOBS FROM HOME

Inside, outside, telemarketing, B2B and consumer sales opportunities

By Laureen Miles Brunelli

This list represents but a small sliver of the sales jobs from home that are available. Sales jobs can very often be a combination of working from home, on-site work and travel, so few sales jobs are advertised as simply "work from home." That said, this list--which includes everything from account exec positions to telemarketing--will give you some ideas and leads, but be sure to search local job ads and job boards for industries in which you have experience.

Also, this list does not include any direct selling opportunities (e.g., Avon) because those are home businesses, not jobs. For more on direct sales, browse this list of <u>direct sales business resources</u>.

For a comprehensive look at what kinds of sales jobs can be done remotely, see this profile:<u>Work at home In Sales</u>.

Alpine Access/SYKES Home

Type of sales job: Telephone (inbound) sales

Industry: BPO

This outsourcing company hires home call center agents as employees in the United States and Canada. The work is mostly customer service but with some inbound sales too. Pays $9 an hour with full- and part-time schedules. Fee for background check is required.

American Express

Type of sales job: Sales rep, sales manager, travel agents

Industry: Financial, travel

While most of American Express's home-based jobs are for virtual travel agents in its Axcess@Home division, which do have a sales aspect to them, the company also has partially and fully work-at-home sales positions in other divisions. Use "virtual," "telecommute" or "work at home" as keywords to find a job online in its database.

ARO

Type of sales job: Telephone sales (inbound)

Industry: BPO

This company offers a wide array of home call center positions in and outside sales, such as teleheath, insurance and customer service. It defines its "TeleSales" positions as "warm" meaning that potential customers called a toll free number or submitted a reply in the mail to wanting more information on this product. Sales experience is required.

Automatic Data Processing (ADP)

Sales, IT, Management, Corporate

Global provider of business processing (payroll, talent management, human resource management, benefits administration and time and attendance to employers and automotive dealerships offers a significant number of home-based opportunities in may different field. Look for jobs in its company database with "home office" in the location.

Balance Your Books

Type of sales job: Business-to-business (B2B), outside

Industry: Outsourced accounting services

Offering the "opportunity to telecommute," accounting outsourcing firm hires sales staff who give presentations on services, solicits new clients and services existing clients. Knowledge of accounting services required.

Best Western International

Type of sales job: Telephone sales (inbound)

Industry: Travel, Call center

Inbound sales representatives in the Beardsley, AZ call center may transition to work at home after six months of acceptable service. Hourly rate is $10-11/hour. Evening hours required. Training is paid; benefits available.

Citizens Financial

Type of sales job: B2B, outside

Industry: Financial services

Financial services company hires home-based sales reps in its auto financing division. Travel required. Use the keyword "remote" in its database.

Cloud 10

Type of sales job: Telephone (inbound)

Industry: BPO, Call center

Hires (as employees) telephone customer service reps, sales agents and technical support people for work-at-home jobs.

Convergys Home Agent Program

Type of sales job: Telephone (inbound)

Industry: BPO, Call center

Virtual call center agents receive incoming calls and provide services that may include customer service, sales or technical support. Convergys offers paid training and benefits for its work at home jobs. See reader reviews of Convergys.

CRUISE.COM

Type of sales job: Telephone (inbound)

Industry: Travel, call center

Home-based support and sales agents at this Internet cruise seller sell cruises and travel insurance. Bilingual in Spanish required for some positions. Bilingual Call Center Jobs

eTutorWorld

Type of sales job: Telemarketing, inside

Industry: Education, call center

Sales associates for eTutorWorld promote online tutoring services in math and science for school students in grades 5 to 12. More Online Teaching Jobs

Extended Presence

Type of sales job: Telephone appointment setting, B2B

Industry: BPO, Call center

Company provides business-to-business phone sales for clients. Agents do cold calling and appointment setting and are paid an hourly base plus incentives.

First Data

Type of sales job: Outside, B2B

Industry: Financial Services

Transaction processing company hires management professionals and account executives to work from home. Multi-tier compensation structure includes a base salary, commissions, residuals, bonuses, and expense reimbursement. Use "remote" in keyword field.

Working Solutions

Type of sales job: Telemarekting

Industry: BPO, call center

BPO contracts with agents to work call center jobs for clients. Pay ranges from $7.20 to $30 anhour.Sales and service projects include enrollments, retail sales, hospitality reservations, and dedicated account support.

FLashBanc

Type of sales job: Inside/outside, business to business

Industry: Credit card

Account executives sell credit card services and equipment to business owners earning commissions and residuals in this position, rather than a salary.

Forest Laboratories

Type of sales job: Outside sales

Industry: Pharmaceutical

Pharmaceutical sales reps work remotely from home but spend much of their time visiting medical offices.

The Hartford

Type of sales job: Outside, business to business

Industry: Insurance

Large insurance company offers work-at-home for many types of positions (nurses, adjusters, attorneys, claims consultants), including sales. Check off "yes" under Remote options and choose "sales" under job function to search the company's job listings. Many of these jobs include extensive travel.

HSN.com

Type of sales job: Telephone sales (inbound)

Industry: Online retail, call center

The Home Shopping Network offers work at home jobs in customer service. Jobs are based in St. Petersburg, FL, Roanoke, VA, and Nashville TN. Inbound calls are both sales and customer service. Full-time positions provide health insurance benefits.

inContact

Type of sales job: Telephone sales (inbound)

Industry: Call center

This company does not actually employ home call center agents, but develops the software for companies that use home call center agents. However, it does have a significant remote workforce in fields such as sales, network operations and software development in the U.S., Canada and other parts of the world.

Intrep

Type of sales job: Inside

Industry: BPO

Company provides sales personnel for its clients. Sales "consultants" generally do B2B appointment setting.

JPMorgan Chase

Type of sales job: Outside sales, business to business (B2B)

Industry: Financial services

Financial institution offers work-from-home positions in sales within its card services division as account execs. These jobs are tied to specific locations, so search job listings using "work at home" but narrowed to your local area.

LiveOps

Type of sales job: Telemarketing (inbound and outbound)

Industry: BPO, call center

Company hires independent-contractor, call-center agents, including licensed insurance agents, for a variety of positions including outbound sales, bilingual customer service and financial services.

Lenovo

Type of sales job: Outside sales, business to business (B2B)

Industry: Technology

Computer manufacturer hires account executive for positions that are 75 percent work at home.

Oracle

Type of sales job: Outside sales, business to business (B2B)

Industry: Technology

Technology giant offers many positions as full-time work from home or with flexible hours that allow work from home, including many of its sales positions based all around the world.

Patch.com/AOL

Type of sales job: Outside, B2B

Industry: Media/advertising, online ad sales

Online local news division of AOL hires work-at-home sales executives and sales managers nationwide.

PayJunction

Type of sales job: Outside sales

Industry: Financial services

Offering paperless transactions in the merchant service industry, company's remote jobs include outside sales in B2B software.

Salesforce.com

Type of sales job: Account executive

Industry: Tech

Customer relationship management (CRM) software firm specializing in social, mobile and cloud technologies hires for work-at-home positions across several divisions including many sales positions

Support.com

Type of sales job: Outside, business to business

Industry: Tech

Support.com provides remote technology services to consumers and small businesses. Many of the support positions in the U.S. and Canada are work at home, and the company has work at home jobs for sales managers in the U. S.

Thomson Reuters

Type of sales job: Outside, business to business

Industry: Finance, law, accounting

Various divisions offer home-based account sales positions with up to 75 percent travel within a specific territory.

WordExpress

Type of sales job: Inside

Industry: Translation

Santa Monica, CA-based company hires full- or part-time freelance sales managers and reps with an "international background" to sell its services and software.

5 Work From Home Telemarketing Companies

By **Alaina Forbes**

Telemarketing may not be for everyone but for those with a sales background who excel at this type of work, this may be the perfect work from home job for you. Duties vary with some companies requiring cold calling while others focus more on customer relationship management.

Blue Zebra

Blue Zebra works with businesses of all sizes performing business to business appointment setting. The entire company is virtual meaning all employees work from home. Work from home agents perform cold calling to set appointments and generate leads. Pay can range from $15 to $25 an hour plus bonuses. Hours are flexible but you must be available four,six or eight hours per day from 8:00 a.m. through 5:00 p.m. ET for five days per week for a total of 20 to 40 hours. Prior outbound calling experience is required. Those interested with no prior experience should start with a different company to gain experience before applying. *See: **BlueZebraAppointmentSetting.com***

TeleSales Specialists

TeleSales Specialists works specifically in the information technology industry . Started in 1996, the company provides telemarketing services to clients computer hardware, software, and telecommunications field. Both part-time and full-time work is available with a flexible schedule ranging from between 10 to 35 hours a week. Pay for work at home telemarketers is $15 an hour. TeleSales Specialists requires agents to have a bachelor's degree or higher plus previous business-to-business or corporate sales experience. *See: **TeleSalesSpecialists.com***

DID YOU KNOW?

Those looking for a work from home job often wonder what the difference is between working for a virtual call center and working in telemarketing. Virtual call centers take mostly inbound calls as opposed to outbound, and while agents may be required to offer up sells, the focus is usually more customer service oriented.

ARO Inc.

ARO inc. works with a variety of industries from insurance to healthcare, performing business process outsourcing. Among the variety of services provided are call center duties, outbound customer relationship management, forms processing, and web-based information solutions. Customer service agents for ARO, will handle both inbound and outbound calls, no cold calling involved. ARO also hires telesales agents responsible for up selling products to a client's customer list. Sales experience is required for these positions. Both part-time and full-time positions are available. *See:* ***ARO Inc.***

Expert Business Development

Expert Business Development, started in 1993, works mostly within the financial industry establishing business to business relationships. Clients include banks, credit unions, financial providers, corporations and entrepreneurial firms. Offering both part-time and full-time positions but requires previous commercial sales experience. *See:* ***ExpertBizDev.com***

Intrep Sales Partners

Intrep focuses on business to business services including appointment setting, lead generation, list acquisition, database management, and administrative support. Sales and marketing background required along with past business experience. You must pass a personality test along with a proficiency test during the application process. Intrep offers a flexible schedule with a per hour wage plus bonuses.*See:* ***Intrep.com***

A sales or business background can help you land one of these flexible work from home jobs. Find one that suits your strengths and further your career from home.

Odesk gave me things I wouldn't be able to afford...

My first Odesk job was a very simple one. It took me just one hour and I gained 100 dollars. I was so excited, thinking this is amazing, I can do tons of money. My enthusiasm was huge and I become in an Odeskserialquoter. First weeks in Odesk I worked a lot waiting and looking offers, quoting and I didn't have success. However in this weeks I discover that there are people with ultra-low rates, the importance of quoting quickly, which is my best hourly rate, and 2 or 3 more

rules that allowed me to gain my second contract for a bet's site from Europe: I remember my sons telling me: Dad, please don't sing this confidential agreement, may be Vito Corleone or Tony Soprano are behind this contract!!!. Again I did it well.

Then after some time I optimized the way I quote, I recognize which offers had value for me, which offers don't.And finally I found a very effective way to write my cover letter. Now I'm happy to say that an important part of my incomes came from Odesk.

Taking the Train in opposite way!!

However Odesk changed other important part of my life. I have a regular job, Monday to Friday 9am to 5pm. Boring, you know. As I live in the suburbs of Buenos Aires, I have to commute 3 hours a day by train and bus, every day!!, In my country trains transport many people, much more people than seats are, of course. So chances to have a seat are near to zero. Well, when I

began to work seriously in Odesk, I had to work many hours to deliver results and of course I need time. So I bought a 3G modem, a notebook and I become the train into my office. There was only one problem to solve yet, how to have a seat (I can't work standing). Well after some analysis my daughter Catalina suggested me to take the train in opposite way (there are a lot of seats in opposite way), then when the train arrives to final station, it bounces it the way I need to travel.

Today I travel more than 3 hours a day, may be 4, however these 4 hours are not wasted time any more, In fact I'm writing this lines on the train. I quoted, worked and closed new jobs from my train office!!

Odeskpays my family vacations!!

In my country the local currency is the Peso, and our local goverment impose to us many Restrictions to buy external currencies like dollars, euros or pesetas. So, I send all Odeskpaymentsto a prepaid debit card (Payoneer) issued in USA.However this card can't be used in ATMs of my country, this is a problem! Moreover, all odesk payment methods don't work in ATMs in Argentina. This is the reason we (my wife, our 4 kids and I) go for vacations to Uruguay, a country where I can use my payoneer card in ATMswithout restrictions. Odesk pays my vacations!!

The Most Important thing Odesk Gave Me

Perhaps many of you have the same feeling, I ever think that I have an unstable work status. I usually think that I can be fired in any moment. Odesk gave me peace, it make me feel really quiet. Because now, having a job depends only on me, no matter what age I am, no matter where I live.I can work with Odesk and produce the money I need to live.

-IgnacioBisso, Argentina-

http://workfromhome.answers.com/call-centers/5-work-from-home-telemarketing-companies

9

VIRTUAL WORK: CLIENT PERSPECTIVE

A Generational Perspective to Managing Virtual Teams

Posted on April 25, 2013 by <u>Giselle Kovary</u>

Making All Generations Comfortable with Working Virtually

These days, working for an organization doesn't necessarily mean heading into an office each day for eight hours or more. In the age of video chats, smartphones, instant messaging, social media and online collaboration, people work from many different locations at many different times. This is not just an employee perk, but a business need. Experts from different geographic areas must come together to solve client challenges and achieve business goals.

However, Traditionalists are used to getting up each morning and going to work, which to them means physically going to a building where work takes place. For most of their careers, they did not work with virtual employees and work was never completed at home. This means that the Traditionalist leaders of today have had to adjust their management styles around virtual or global teams. The traditional methods of managing employees (observing employees at their desks, making sure everyone comes in and leaves on time, ensuring that office rules and policies are followed, etc.) no longer work when teams are spread out across the country or the globe. Traditionalist leaders need to focus on outcomes and results instead of 'face time.'

Baby Boomers see working from home as a privilege, not a right. Many Baby Boomers believe that only high performers or those with a great deal of seniority should be able to work remotely as a reward for their service. However, the construction of global virtual teams is no longer a luxury. It has now become a necessity and Baby Boomers have had to adapt.

Working Remotely with Traditionalist & Baby Boomer Employees

In many organizations, Traditionalist employees may be expected to work remotely along with other colleagues. Its best for leaders to provide Traditionalists with a lot of direction when creating a virtual team, especially at first. Traditionalists often aren't accustomed to completing work on a less defined schedule. In addition, since they won't be able to physically express their dedication and hard work, they'll need to know how their managers and the organization will measure their success.

Baby Boomers who are part of virtual teams often want to build credibility to ensure that they are well-positioned in the team and that they are able to add value. They may struggle with how to build strong relationships if there is limited ability to meet face-to-face. Using highly interactive technology such as video conferences, real time chats and other tools will ensure an engaging experience for all team members.

Gen X, Gen Y and Virtual teams

Gen Xers and Gen Ys are quick to adapt to virtual team environments and often request for this type of team structure. Gen Xers who lead virtual teams are often very effective because they adopt a results-based approach. They don't focus on how or when work is completed, but rather if the work is produced correctly and delivered on time.

Gen Ys have participated in virtual teams for most of their lives. They are very comfortable with collaborating online and likely have formed relationships with people they rarely (if ever) meet face-to-face. However, Gen Ys may struggle with the fact that some members of a virtual team may not be as comfortable in using online tools as their primary form of communication. Be prepared to receive feedback and suggestions from Gen Y team members on how technology can be better leveraged to increase collaboration.

For more details on leading virtual teams, please see chapter 6 in Upgrade Now: 9 Advanced Leadership Skills available at www. ngenperformance.com/book.

http://www.ngenperformance.com/blog/hr-training/a-generational-perspective-to-managing-virtual-teams

Keeping Virtual Teams Real: Successfully Managing Off-site Staff

by Phyllis Cartwright, RHIA, CCS

For managers of staff who work off-site, good communication is the key to establishing more than a remote connection. Gone are casual practices such as "management by walking around."

HIM departments understand firsthand the need to tap into talent across geographic boundaries, and many already benefit from advances in networking and collaborative technology. Over the past decade, working remotely from home, client sites, regional offices, and on the road have become common work arrangements.

Those advances are reconfiguring HIM departments, creating teams comprised of staff who work on- and off-site. In other departments, staff may be entirely remote. Managers must adapt in order to effectively lead cohesive, high-performing teams in the new virtual workplace.

That's not always easy. The physical separation of manager and staff challenges many traditional management techniques. Gone are practices such as "management by walking around."

Virtual offices change how people communicate and work with each other, transfer information, establish authority and rules, and perform and measure performance. Although emerging collaboration, networking, and remote-access technologies provide the IT infrastructure for a virtual workplace, changes in organizational culture and behavior are the key to its ultimate success.

Are You There?: Managing by Results, Not Scrutiny

It can be deceptive to gauge productivity by appearance. In traditional offices, smart managers know that is an easy error to make—assuming that one staffer is hard at work because he is at his desk while assuming that another is goofing off because she isn't.

Managers of virtual teams make the same error if they assume that off-site staff are not at work when they don't pick up the phone or reply immediately to e-mail. That's why managing by results (or objectives) is fundamental with virtual teams.

Managing by results begins with communicating clear goals, setting deadlines and sticking to them, and measuring accomplishments against those expectations.

Real Communication for Virtual Staff

Successful remote workers are disciplined and self-motivated; however, they do not want to be ignored. Poor communication is one of the most common complaints of virtual employees, and it often is caused by a lack of interaction with the manager or other team members.

Virtual staff need contact with their coworkers and managers to maximize productivity, quality, and a sense of community. Managers must find the right mix of technology and communication to provide remote staff with the connection they need.

Organizations that rely on virtual workers have four main areas of management concern: building trust; establishing commitment; ensuring self-efficacy; and managing communication among the virtual work force. Strong communication is at the heart of each issue.

Trust is the key to any relationship, but it's particularly important for managers and staff who don't see each other daily. Just as in an office, if an employee doesn't immediately answer the phone doesn't mean that the person is goofing around. Remote staff are entitled to a lunch hour, breaks, and trips to the restroom, just as office-based staff are. Being within sight does not guarantee staff are being productive. Managers need only recall the many distractions in a traditional office—surfing the Web, e-mailing friends, and visiting colleagues at their cubicles.

Managers must remember that employees were hired to perform specific jobs and that the results are more important than the settings. Managing staff by results is critical in a virtual setting, and managers should focus on what's accomplished.

Clear Expectations, Consistent Communication

All staff, whether on- or off-site, rely on clearly defined goals to direct and measure their work. For staff working off-site, communicating those expectations fully is especially crucial. A great amount of information is communicated informally in office settings—through hallway conversations and chats at a cubicle.

Remote staff deserve that same access, and providing them with full and current information requires a more organized effort. Managers should document project expectations, changes, and updates in writing and distribute them via e-mail or fax.

Most coding professionals now working remotely, for example, once worked on-site at a hospital. There, deciphering clinical documentation and coding puzzles was made easier by walking to the next cubicle and consulting with a colleague. Now, coding in more isolated surroundings requires creative solutions to maintain coding quality, monitor productivity, and staff appropriately.

Collaborative technologies that allow for document sharing and shared project tracking help keep everyone in the loop. Good use of teleconferences, e-mail, and instant messaging can boost connectivity with coworkers and managers. Webinars and interactive online software enable staff to see the same presentation whether on-site or off.

As helpful as these technologies are, managers must be highly organized and adept at communicating both in writing and over the phone. Managers once familiar with keeping the lines of communication open by stopping by offices throughout the day are seeking new ways to replicate that interaction virtually.

Regularly scheduled conference calls are essential. They help managers understand if the expected results are on target and, if not, whether adjustments or further discussions are needed. New staff in particular benefit from regularly scheduled check-ins to discuss their work and progress. Consistent communication also lets the new hire know that the manager is accessible.

Regular contact is also important to maintain staff morale. In a traditional office setting, it is easy to compliment someone by stopping at his or her office to say "good job." For off-site employees, acknowledgment can require more effort. Sending a simple e-mail or picking up the phone to say "I'm thinking of you and the high quality work you've done lately" can make a world of difference to a remote worker.

In addition to investing in adequate IT, companies must have an IT department capable of clearly communicating with virtual employees through any tech crisis. Companies should also have a plan for troubleshooting an employee's computer, quickly recovering important files, and overnight delivery of new equipment when necessary.

Choosing the Right Jobs, the Right Staff, the Right Managers

Before any day-to-day managing begins, the fundamental management challenge of virtual teams is selecting the HIM functions that can successfully move into a virtual environment.

The most suitable functions to have made the virtual jump to date are coding and transcription. From a management perspective, coding and transcription professionals work very independently, based on clearly defined expectations. Their functions are well suited for independent work while maintaining work output, quality, and delivery.

Managers must also identify the appropriate skills, experience, and necessary behavioral competencies for staff who will perform work off-site, independently, without compromising their performance level or work satisfaction. This presents a paradigm shift from traditional staff management.

In general, individuals who display a high degree of teamwork and collaboration and don't suffer from the loss of social networking, visibility, and being in the center of action prove to be the best fit for the virtual workplace.

New Skills for Managers

Virtual workplaces also require specific skills and characteristics from managers. Managers accustomed to traditional settings can become frustrated by the difficulties associated with a virtual work force, such as the inability to resolve issues face-to-face and perceived problems in maintaining accountability. Recruiting and retaining the right manager with the correct blend of skills and experience to direct and motivate a virtual team is imperative for the department's success.

As a manager, the very real barriers of not having face-to-face interactions with staff requires a high degree of organization and communication skills that are effective in either written or verbal forms.

Managers may need to change their perceptions and beliefs on how they manage, motivate, and influence to succeed in a virtual work setting. Virtual teams may require new methods for measuring individual and team performance. Without defined expectations against which to benchmark performance, unreal expectations can build, causing doubts about the remote working practice as a whole. Virtual managers also may need to expand their communication skills, because they will be challenged to keep their staff motivated as a team and to let them know long-distance that they are valued by the organization.

Managing the new workplace also requires flexibility and a sharp eye. Virtual teams commonly face unique process issues involving workflow, quality auditing and reporting, analysis, monitoring production and work output, staffing (including covering for vacation or unscheduled time away from work), and access to on-site liaisons or support staff to support the virtual manager's tasks.

For instance, a virtual coder assigned to coding inpatient records will require a way to communicate with physicians and assign query forms as well as site support to get the expected outcome of response and resolution. For these reasons managers require a sharp eye to identify potential workflow issues and create work-arounds for daily activities, and they must approach their work with adaptability and creativity.

Measuring Program Success

HIM professionals must assess the effectiveness of the program and position organizations for improved operational performance. In using this approach, managers can select a blend of short-term and long-term quantitative and qualitative measures of success.

Expected short-term quantitative measures would include productivity (e.g., if remote staff have sufficient hardware and connectivity to accomplish the required work for each assignment). From a long-term perspective, managers must provide the support necessary to ensure that high-quality technology is available to the virtual work force. From a qualitative perspective, both short- and long-term measures are validated through stable high-quality work, the goal of every HIM department, no matter where its staff work.

Managing Privacy and Security in Remote Departments

Resources in the FORE Library: HIM Body of Knowledge

An important part of managing virtual staff is managing the secure and confidential exchange of protected health information. As information becomes more fluid and technology becomes more robust, nearly every type of medical, financial, and administrative data can be accessed and shared remotely.

Recent Journal articles address considerations in managing remote technologies to reduce risk and meet compliance regulations:

"Weighing the Pros and Cons of IM: Instant Messaging Offers Instant Conveniences, Instant Complications," September 2007

"Safeguards for Remote Access," July–August 2007

"Mobile Device Use, Reuse, and Disposal," June 2007

"Connectivity, Privacy, and Liability: What Medical Professionals Must Consider," April 2007

Read these and other articles related to off-site staff, business associates, privacy, and security in the FORE Library: HIM Body of Knowledge at www.ahima.org. *Phyllis Cartwright* *(pcartwright@precysesolutions.com) is director of remote coding at Precyse Solutions, LLC.*

Article citation:

Cartwright, Phyllis. "Keeping Virtual Teams Real: Successfully Managing Off-site Staff." *Journal of AHIMA* 78, no.9 (October 2007): 26-32.

http://library.ahima.org/xpedio/groups/public/documents/ ahima/bok1_035526.hcsp?dDocName=bok1_035526

THE REALITY OF VIRTUAL WORKERS; AN INTERVIEW WITH UK ACCOUNTANTS, RICHARD PLACE DOBSON

by **helencousins** on January 27th, 2012

Technology has given rise to many possibilities for digital business; the global market, the paperless office, and the virtual worker to name but a few. But are these simply aspirations for SMEs or are they a reality already?

*Well, UK accountancy practice, <u>Richard Place Dobson</u> has long since embraced the paperless office and for the past three months one of their senior practice accountants, Jennifer Watson, has worked for this UK firm from her home in the south-east of Ireland. **This interview looks at how virtual working actually works, both from the perspective of the employer and the employee.***

The New World of Work

In 2011, <u>Microsoft commissioned a study</u> which interviewed 1,500 workers across 15 European countries on their attitudes towards flexible working. This study led Microsoft to develop their thinking on the workplace of the future, entitled "The New World of Work.

In practical terms, Microsoft believes that we are moving very quickly from flexible working to a New World of Work, in which redesigned offices and the latest technology facilitate even greater flexibility. This makes our working lives easier and more manageable. This New World of Work as envisaged by Microsoft is about people, places and technology and we look at how this all pans out in real life in the interview below.

First, I interviewed Philip Hayden, a Director of Richard Place Dobson.

Tell me a little bit about the practice, Philip.

We are located in Crawley, West Sussex in England. The firm has four directors and a further twenty-four employees. Our services are fairly typical for an accountancy firm in general practice. We offer services in relation to accounts, audit, tax, bookkeeping, payroll, start-ups, business plans and charities. Our clients are mainly in the areas of engineering, construction, professional services and consultants. While our services are typical, we like to think that we offer a more caring and personal service to our clients.

Is your accounts production and tax calculation software based in the cloud?

All of our software is server based, except Microsoft Outlook, which is cloud based. Standard software packages are used for corporation tax, personal tax, accounts preparation, bookkeeping, payroll, document management, and audit as well as our own time recording. We consider ourselves a paperless office, so accounts working papers are computerised as well. We can link from our own working papers right back into client PDF documents. Our working papers are standardised templates, so it streamlines the accounts preparation process and provides a really good audit trail. This means we can easily see where we derived our figures from.

How did Jennifer come to work for you from Ireland?

Jennifer is Irish and had trained and worked in Ireland before she starting working for us in 2010. She was working with us, for one year, when she came and told us that she had to move back to Ireland for personal reasons.

We didn't want to lose her, and she didn't particularly want to leave us, so we asked her if she would like to become a virtual worker, and work from her home in Ireland. Jennifer would have spent a lot of time in her first year here being trained in our work flow system as well as in the software that we use, and of course, she had to learn about the UK taxation system, which differs significantly from the Irish system. It's a highly skilled job, and both the firm and our employees invest considerable time and effort into being trained to simply do the job well.

What were the practicalities of setting Jennifer up to work remotely from Ireland?

We set her up with a computer, printer and scanner to take home and we remoted this to her original machine here, (which we keep running in our communications room). She can access her machine here in the same way that she could when she was here and because all our files are computer based she can access anything on the system as before. If we need to send information to her, (documents or papers of any kind), these are scanned and sent by email.

How do you keep in touch with Jennifer?

Apart from email, we use Skype with video so that she can have a face to face conversation with anyone here to discuss any aspects of her work or about her clients. We also set up a link from our phone system so that when clients call and want to speak to Jennifer they can be put straight through to her machine in Ireland via Skype.

Jennifer is also able to be present, (via Skype), at our monthly team meetings.

Does Jennifer ever come into the office in the UK?

Jennifer will come over to do her CPD studies on average not more than once a month so will call into the office then. She worked at the office last week to deal with some special work and will be coming over again shortly to help with a special project for a client.

How do you think the virtual working arrangement is working out?

This was a new venture for us but so far seems to be working very well and is a lot better than having to recruit someone else, paying agency fees and a considerable investment of time and money for training. Small issues crop up from time to time but so far nothing we can't deal with.

Have you had virtual workers in the past, and if so, what is different this time?

Four or five of our workers have continual remote access so they can work from home if need be during busy periods i.e. currently during the tax season or when the weather is particularly bad e.g. last year when we had lots of snow and they could not otherwise get to the office. Jennifer is the first person we have had work permanently from home – because of the remoteness.

Some of our other UK based staff can access their desktop machines remotely from home if the need arises, which has proved useful at very busy times, and when they have been marooned at home in the snow. This didn't take much to set up and can usually be done remotely. One key person was stuck at home during a very busy period without remote access but we were able to get him up and running within an hour or so. Log in is via a secure <u>Virtual Private Network</u>, (VPN), link.

Has Jennifer had to change her client portfolio to facilitate this new working arrangement?

It has been necessary to make minor changes but she mainly works on the same clients.

Are your clients aware of the arrangement and if so, what has their reaction been?

We have decided not to make any announcement to our clients. Not that it needs to be a secret but there is basically no difference to the way the service is provided.

How can a virtual worker maintain a career path to attain promotion?

We haven't got that far yet.

Can you tell us what the main advantages of virtual workers are for your firm?

In this case it saved having to recruit, but it also saves office space, which is at a premium.

Would you consider extending the virtual workforce in the future?

Yes, with the right person.

What are the disadvantages?

There don't seem to be many. Obviously it's easier if someone can be physically present sometimes but I am not aware of any frustrations here. You need to have the infrastructure and without a "paperless office" it would be much harder to implement.

Next, I interviewed Jennifer Watson, who is working remotely from Ireland for UK accountants, Richard Place Dobson. [Disclosure: Jennifer is my niece].

Have you got a work routine?

Yes. My working hours are the exact same as when I was in the office, I have an hour for lunch. One of the main reasons for this is so that it doesn't affect the client or my colleagues when they want to contact me.

Do you find it difficult to separate your life from your work now that you work from home?

It was a bit strange at first, but now I have set up a room in my house purely as my office which helps keep my home life separate.

What are the main challenges that you face, now that you are not in an office with your colleagues?

I don't really see any challenge to not being in the office. I can have face to face contact with my colleagues through Skype; my work is scanned to me, (which was usually the case when I was in the office). If I have to meet with clients, these can be scheduled for when I am back in the office each month.

What effect does remote working have on your productivity?

Other than the initial set up time which was involved, the only effect has been positive. I actually find my productivity has gone up as I don't have any of the general office distractions.

Does the equipment or your broadband ever let you down, and how does it affect your work?

So far my equipment has not let me down. If for example I have a power cut, I will make up my hours once it comes back on, (what-ever the time).

Does the constant travel between England and Ireland pose any challenges?

I go over to the office once a month. I usually travel very early in the morning or late at night, in order that I don't miss any working hours. The travel hours are quite long, however my normal commute to work is quite short, (up the stairs!), and so it balances out really.

Jennifer, I know that you were delighted to be able to continue with your current job in the UK even though you had to return to Ireland to live. Three months on, how are things going for you as a remote worker?

I love it. It was a bit strange at first being out of the office, but now that I have gotten used to it, it couldn't be better. I really appreciate what Richard Place Dobson has done for me. I enjoy working with them and I hope I can be a great asset for them. Above all, it has provided me with a job that doesn't depend on the Irish economy!

Would you recommend to others to consider remote or virtual work?

Yes definitely. It's a great way for firms to save on day to day office costs (e.g. building insurance or rent), while increasing productivity of the worker. Also it might help with the recruitment of staff, in that you could look outside your area and potential staff will not have to relocate.

Thanks to Philip and Jennifer for sharing their real-life experience of the virtual workforce. Virtual working seems to be worthwhile from both the perspective of employee and employer, where a role lends itself to that. One might not expect an accountancy practice, a business type which is usually seen as conservative, to use virtual working successfully. Yet, it makes perfect sense to do so, at least in this case.

http://tweakyourbiz.com/technology/2012/01/27/the-reality-of-virtual-workers-an-interview-with-uk-accountants-richard-place-dobson/

7 Things Freelancers Should Know About How Clients View Freelance Work

Ever wonder what your clients are thinking? Wish you could get inside their heads and find out what drives them? Showing that you are perceptive and understand client wants and needs can help you stand out and receive more quality work from them in the future.

At Work Market we spend a lot of time talking to companies who hire freelance workers. We asked them for what makes the perfect freelancer. The following are seven key tips to making clients happy (and getting more work) - straight from the source.

1. **Uphold the client's brand.** If your project is onsite, maintain professionalism and procure necessary information about the project and the brand prior to arriving onsite. Dress professionally, arrive on time and come prepared with all required equipment and tools. You are the face of their brand and are expected to act courteously and well-informed. This generally results in repeat business and strong ratings, which then brings more projects for both you and the client.

2. **Companies do not use contractors just to save money.** Benefits behind using a freelance workforce

reach beyond saving money on their overhead. Other advantages include an increase in quality and productivity, the expansion of coverage nationally or even globally, or as a reaction to the growing number of people who choose to work as independent contractors. Help them in these regards and you won't find yourself in bidding wars.

Know the client. Book the job.

3. **Continue to evolve.** More workers are seeing the benefits of going freelance. An increase in the "talent pool" means an increase in competition. It is more important than ever to maintain skills and certifications. Clients want you to evolve as well. You

have to so you do not fall behind. Invest in training and education to stay ahead of the curve.

4. **Competition is increasing for buyers.** Believe it or not, increased competition also holds true on client side as more companies are discovering the advantages in utilizing an on-demand workforce. This means a boost in quality jobs for the best of the best. This also means better pay and honest ratings. Why? Clients know they will miss out on quality contract workers if they do not prove themselves to be fair. They want to make it easy for you to work with them. Using online staffing marketplaces, like Work Market, and a fully functioning mobile application are two ways they can do just that.

5. **Go mobile.** Soon enough, all work will be managed and conducted over your mobile device. If you do not have a smartphone yet, get one. If you have not downloaded a client's app yet, do it now. Clients want their onsite workforce to have the ability to upload required documents and obtain signatures while on location. They know that mobile is the workforce solution of the future. You simply have to be there.

6. **Be a business.** Cultivate a professional identity to stand out to clients looking for a contractor. Trademark your business. Get insurance. Enhance your LinkedIn page. Since they will never meet you, presenting yourself as a serious professional online will lessen any hesitation they might have in conducting business transactions with you.

7. **Clients want to build a relationship with you.** Securing trust from a client leads to higher ratings and

can help in getting references, both which help you attain more work. Gain trust by performing consistent, quality work and communicating effectively both during and upon completion of a project.

http://blog.workmarket.com/post/76322556206/7-things-freelancers-should-know-about-how-clients-view

THE WAY YOU WORK: JOSHUA WARREN'S JOURNEY FROM ODESK FREELANCER TO THRIVING CLIENT

The Way We Work

October 23, 2013 by <u>Catherine Raney</u>

With experience both as an oDesk freelancer and client, Joshua Warren has a unique perspective on online work.

It all started when the economy took a dive several years ago. He found steady work on oDesk as a freelance web developer earning $15/hour, but in no time he was commanding a rate of $95/hr—and still the demand for his work was more than he could keep up with. As a result, he began hiring other oDesk freelancers to help with overflow work.

Still, the requests kept on coming, and Joshua soon realized he couldn't get all of this work done by himself. He recalls, "I was just a single freelancer getting absolutely overwhelmed with the amount of work, and realized that I needed help. Instead of looking for someone locally, I wanted to find the absolute best person that could help me no matter where they were in the world."

So, in 2008 Joshua founded <u>Creatuity</u>, a web development firm specializing in Magento, PHP and WordPress. He explains how he got started: "I found a project, just a personal project that I hadn't made a lot of progress on and didn't have a lot of time for. I put it out there as a test project and hired a few different people. That's actually how I ended up finding someone that I'm still working with to this day."

Flash forward five years, and Joshua is at the helm of a booming business that currently employs 23 people, 13 of which are remote and deliver all work online. While growing his company, he honed his own best practices for hiring and managing online talent. Below are five of our favoriteoDesk success strategies from Joshua.

1. Don't narrow your talent search by hourly rate—the perfect freelancer might be out there for just a little bit more.

Because getting it done right is usually more important than getting it done cheaply, Joshua advises against narrowing your applicant pool based on hourly rate. He explains that when he first started hiring online, he discovered that "instead of finding the best balance between price and quality, a lot of people were just looking for the best price. I realized that it's important to get as many candidates as possible by not narrowing down on money upfront and leaving the job requirements open." This technique has helped Joshua identify a number of talented freelancers who—while a little more expensive—were well worth the investment.

2. Look for candidates who are passionate about what they do and who you'll personally enjoy working with.

When it comes to evaluating potential hires, Joshua has developed his own formula based on equal parts communication and passion. He explains, "Finding someone I can work well with can be just as important as finding someone with the technical qualifications, so I'll look to see if they included something about themselves in their application. Did they say something that shows me they're passionate about what they do, that they are interested in it, that this isn't just another contract and another few hundred dollars? Is this something that is their craft, that they enjoy doing? Those are the people that stand out to me, and those will usually be the very first ones I'll invite to interview."

> Our clients are amazed because they will bring us something at 5:00 p.m. and they're thinking 'Hey, you know, it's 5:00 p.m. here in Dallas, we're going home and it's going to be a little while before I hear back on this.' We'll hand it off to someone in Poland, and by the time the client is back in the office at 8:00 a.m. the work is done. The clients are just blown away because they think someone was up all night working on it!"

3. Written communication is a key indicator of overall job performance.

With online work, Joshua has found that there is a strong correlation between written skills and overall performance. This is because the most common way for remote team members to work together is through email or other written messages. For this reason, Joshua explains that "you need someone who isn't afraid to send you a detailed daily email, and who will also understand you when you reply." To identify people who can communicate well in writing, Joshua focuses on written abilities instead of verbal abilities in his interviews.

4. Establish and articulate a clear company culture to guide your hiring and management decisions.

Joshua disagrees with the common misconception that you can't create a company culture with remote workers. So, one day he and his team developed a list of their core values using email and online polls. He explains, "it really surprised everyone we had hired because they'd never seen remote workers treated that way—they were used to being treated as these contractors that you kind of use up on a project and then move onto the next thing." This experience proved to Joshua that building a company culture with your remote team is not only possible, but also has a strong positive impact on things like team morale and engagement. He explains, "I think it's helped more with retention than bonuses or raises or anything else really could."

5. Double your productivity (and gain a killer competitive advantage) by building a network of global freelancers to cover all time zones.

In Joshua's experience, having a team from many different time zones is smart business strategy. Creatuity is currently running at 18 hours of productivity per 24-hour cycle, and Joshua plans on recruiting in China, Australia, and Japan to get that productivity rate up to 100% of the day. He explains the benefits of having a company that never stops working: "Our clients are amazed because they will bring us something at 5:00 p.m. and they're thinking 'Hey, you know, it's 5:00 p.m. here in Dallas, we're going home and it's going to be a little while before I hear back on this.' We'll hand it off to someone in Poland, and by the time the client is back in the office at 8:00 a.m. the work is done. The clients are just blown away because they think someone was up all night working on it!"

For more about Joshua and his best practices, check out our free eBook or our Client Resource Center!

https://www.odesk.com/blog/2013/10/way-work-joshua-warrens-journey-odesk-freelancer-thriving-client/

A Client's Perspective: 3 Key Ways to Stand Out as a Freelance Blogger

December 3, 2013 By **Tom Ewer**

In December 2011, I quit my job and started blogging for a living. I blogged on a freelance basis for a variety of clients, eventually snagging rates of $150+ per hour.

However, over the past few months I have switched over to a subcontracting business model, where I play a more editorial role, paying other freelancers to write blog content which I then review for quality and send on to clients.

This situation puts me in the unique situation of seeing both sides of the coin. While <u>I know what it's like to be a freelance blogger</u>, **I also know what it's like to work *with* freelance bloggers**. Becoming a "client" to freelance bloggers has given me a far better understanding of the key characteristics of successful freelancers. Here are the three key lessons I've learned.

1. Being a good writer isn't enough

Let's start with the obvious: you need to be a good writer to succeed as a freelancer. Nobody will hire you if you can't produce great content for their blog. But being a great writer is just the price of entry.

You can think of freelance blogging as a fairground where you have to pay to get in but also pay to ride the attractions. You'll need more than just your entrance ticket to have fun (i.e. get paid a good rate).

What does this mean for you? **Most freelance bloggers need to demonstrate <u>a wide range of skills</u> in order to earn the best rates.** It's simply not enough to just be able to write.

For bloggers specifically, you must demonstrate that you can blog. By far the best way to do this is to run your own relatively successful blog. Doing so will give you valuable experience and serve as a source of samples to woo future clients.

Clients often favor <u>active social media accounts</u> as well, as they like to see you sharing their content and giving it an extra boost. This fact just helps to illustrate the basic truth that you can always do well to think of freelancing in terms of what you can do to benefit the client.

Additionally, <u>copywriting</u> and <u>marketing</u> skills are coveted. If you can write an article and help the client put together an effective promotion strategy, you'll never be left wanting for work.

2. Little things matter

Clients don't value your writing in a vacuum; they are paying you for specific services that they believe will increase their bottom line. That makes it an imperative that, as a freelance writer, you **present a solution to the client — not a problem**.

In my experience, many freelancers don't appreciate this. While they may offer a solution to some extent, that solution is often riddled with problems that take time to resolve.

The most obvious example of this is a poorly edited post: one that contains typos and grammatical errors. You'd be surprised by how many submissions I have received where the writer simply didn't bother to proofread.

A client is hiring you so that they don't have to worry about writing. If they have to go through each article you submit with a fine-tooth comb, it rather defeats the purpose of hiring a writer in the first place. You should always place a premium on quality in your work, because clients don't want anything less. Taking that extra step to ensure that your article is fully polished may not seem like a big deal, but it makes a huge difference to a client.

Personally speaking, I have only worked with a couple of writers who I simply know I don't have to check. For the rest, I know that I have to make sure that typos, strangely-worded sentences and grammatical oddities haven't slipped through the net.

What I would give to receive a piece and know that I could just send it straight onto the client! **I would happily pay more for that**, but such qualities are extremely rare.

The moral of the story should be obvious: **if you focus on providing well-polished posts, you will be in high demand**.

I'm not saying that you need to be perfect; everybody has an occasional typo here and there, but you can certainly strive for perfection. If you work to make each blog post you pen as perfect as possible, your clients will be pleased and you will be paid.

3. Poor professional skills can sink you

Here's the hard truth: **how you conduct yourself is absolutely vital to your success**. And here's the sad reality: many freelance writers don't fully appreciate that fact.

As I've said, good writing can only take you so far, after which your momentum will peter out. So let's put aside the whole writing thing for a moment and just focus on your "professional skills," by which I mean things like your reliability, organization and communication.

Remember that you should always aim to provide a solution, not a problem. If we consider this fact, it becomes readily apparent that being late on deadlines or failing to respond promptly to emails makes you a problem.

Of course you can't always be at your client's beck and call. But **you *should*be responsive to them and you *should* always deliver on what you promise**(acts of God and the like excepted). One of many ways to effectively do this is to learn how to <u>manage your time</u>.

If you can't get organized, communicate well and remain a reliable writer, clients will become wary. Nobody wants to work with someone who constantly makes excuses and turns in assignments late. Don't use an existing lack of organizational skills as an excuse — sort it out.

Conclusion

You may read through the above tips and consider them simple. Well, they are — I won't apologize for that. Nobody ever said that success had to be complicated.

At the end of the day, it's about doing the simple things right.

If you communicate efficiently, create quality pieces on time and bring more to the table than just a written article, you will be coveted by your existing clients and sought out by prospective clients. When that happens, you'll know that you stand out.

How have you endeared yourself to your clients?

http://thewritelife.com/a-clients-perspective-3-key-ways-to-stand-out-as-a-freelance-blogger/

A CLIENT PERSPECTIVE ON FREELANCE BIDDING SITES

AUGUST 23, 2012*by* JAKE POINIER

A friend, Betty, was looking for a **freelance graphic designer** to help her with the second generation of her small business website; unfortunately, the two design contacts I gave her weren't able to help out. Before asking me for additional recommendations, Betty sought out one of the most popular internet freelance bidding sites. The winning bidder offered to create a logo for $100.

It was, quite simply, a disaster:

- The winning bidder had a great-looking portfolio, but the first designs he sent her were garbage.
- After another round of garbage, she became suspicious that the logos in his portfolio weren't even his creations.

- He was based in Yemen. (Not that there's anything wrong with that, but you're taking your chances with an overseas vendor.)
- Betty wasted a lot of time and energy, and is no closer to having a logo than she was 2 weeks ago.

As a client, she experienced exactly what I could have predicted. I tried to be gentle about saying, "Gee, Betty, what did you expect for $100?"

So, how can this client perspective help freelancers improve their business? I'm not going to say, "Never use freelance bidding sites," because that's between you, your bank account, and your deity of choice. But it is certainly an argument to be mindful of a couple of things:

- You're competing on price, not <u>talent</u>.
- You're competing against an unknown volume of people—and market logic dictates that the better the project, the larger the volume.
- You may be competing against people who are unscrupulous, and put things in their portfolios that aren't their own original work in order to win.
- Even if you win, you may lose. I don't feel sorry for the "winning" bidder, but he didn't get paid a cent for whatever time he spent on it, since Betty rejected his work.

If you want to make money freelancing, you need to get beyond bidding sites and their ugly cousins, the content mills. You can find freelance jobs that go beyond "<u>the real minimum wage</u>," but it takes a little work, ingenuity and persistence. For starters, head to JennMattern's great suggestions in a post this week for those freelancers interested in **Moving Beyond Penny Per Word Writing Gigs**. Read it, and heed it.

http://deardrfreelance.com/2012/08/a-client-perspective-on-freelance-bidding-sites/